Annabel Karmel

princess party

cookbook

over 100 delicious recipes and fun ideas

EBURY PRESS

To my two princesses Lara and Scarlett

10 9 8 7 6 5 4 3 2 1

Published in 2009 by Ebury Press, an imprint of Ebury Publishing
A Random House Group Company

The Random House Group Limited Reg. No. 954009

Addresses for companies within the Random House Group can be found at
www.randomhouse.co.uk

A CIP catalogue record for this book is available from the British Library

The Random House Group Limited supports The Forest Stewardship Council (FSC),
the leading international forest certification organisation. All our titles that are printed
on Greenpeace approved FSC certified paper carry the FSC logo. Our paper procurement
policy can be found at www.rbooks.co.uk/environment

To buy books by your favourite authors and register for offers visit www.rbooks.co.uk

Printed and bound by Firmengruppe APPL, Wemding, Germany
Colour origination by Altaimage, London

Design & illustrations: Smith & Gilmour Ltd, London
Photography: Dave King
Food stylist: Seiko Hatfield
Props stylist: Jo Harris
Copy editor: Helena Caldon

Special thanks to Adrienne D' Souza at A Party Palace, 487–493 Upper Richmond
Road West, East Sheen, London SW14 7PU (www.apartypalace.co.uk) for the loan
of props and costumes used in this book.

ISBN 9780091925086

contents

Introduction **4**

Make-up and Jewellery **8**

Valentine's Day **22**

Easter Princess **36**

Movie Star Sleepover **52**

Princess Soda Fountain **68**

Princess Flower Fairies **88**

Princess Beach Babe **104**

The Princess and the Pea **120**

Christmas Angels **134**

Index **156**

About the Author **159**

once upon a time there was a little princess...

And every little girl deserves to eat like royalty. So welcome to this wonderful collection of easy and inspiring ideas that has been specially created to feed your little princess's imagination.

Combine these deliciously simple recipes with your little girl's dreams and together you can enjoy an enchanted afternoon creating magical dishes every day, and even make decorations and accessories for themed parties.

There's nothing a princess likes more than throwing a party, and with this book the preparation for it can be just as much fun as the party itself. With nine themes to choose from there is something here to please every princess. For example, why not have a Make-up and Jewellery Party? You could set the scene by making hand-held mirrors from coloured card with jewelled handles as the invitation, then get your little princess involved in preparing a royal banquet with sparkling ruby mocktails, emerald pizzas and jewelled cupcakes. At the party all the girls can make decorative bracelets and necklaces from beads or edible ones from pasta, fruit and other treats. Each girl could even have a mini makeover to transform her into a stunning cover-girl princess and then have her photograph taken wearing a jewelled tiara, which you can send to her after the party.

With the simplest ingredients you can help your child indulge her fantasies in the sanctuary of home. By doing so she'll learn how to measure out ingredients, discover how fun it is to create great home-made food, and enjoy the mouthwatering results of her work. The recipes are so tasty you may want to serve them up at adult dinner parties too...

Cinema-style nachos and crunchy caramel popcorn make a magical midnight feast for a sleepover, or cook seraphim's sticky salmon and Cinderella coach risotto to turn an everyday family supper into a royal banquet; then with heart-shaped cookies and Little Red Velvet Cakes you can make baking together a Royal Family Affair.

By empowering your child to live out her dreams and by nurturing her vivid imagination, you can help her discover more about who she really is. And helping your child learn to make and enjoy home-made dishes gives her a wonderful start to a lifetime of loving good food.

So, fill your home with the aroma of delicious cooking, the sound of giggling princesses dashing and dancing, and the sight of your little girl enjoying a truly magical childhood.

Every girl – big or little – needs to release her inner princess now and then. So, by royal appointment, enjoy...

Annabel Karmel

make-up
and jewellery

emerald pizzas

Little ladies like to nibble dainty snacks whilst enjoying their salon sessions. Thin and crisp pizzas spread with emerald pesto and studded with tasty morsels fit the bill. If you are making large numbers of these, it may be better to bake a couple of pizzas at a time and serve wedges of those while more are baking.

Makes 4 pizzas (easily increased)
4 wheat tortilla wraps or ready-made
   pizza bases
2–3 tbsp basil pesto
200 g (7 oz) cherry tomatoes,
   thinly sliced
170 g (6 oz) grated mozzarella
   (or if you prefer, half mozzarella
   and half Cheddar)
Optional toppings
8 olives, thinly sliced
4 thin slices ham, cut into squares
55 g (2 oz) Red Leicester cheese,
   cut into squares

★ Pre-heat the oven to 200°C/400°F/Gas 6. Sit the wraps or pizza bases on 2 large baking sheets and spread a thin layer of pesto over the surface of each. Arrange the sliced tomatoes on top of the pesto and scatter over the mozzarella.

★ Add any extra toppings the children have chosen and bake for 8–10 minutes, until the cheese is golden and bubbling and the wraps or pizza bases are brown and crisp.

golden nuggets

Golden, crunchy nuggets of chicken are likely to be added to any princess's list of treasures. Serve them with the Tomato or Maple Mustard Dip (below), or both, and try them with Skinny Oven Chips (page 73).

Makes 8 portions

450 g (1 lb) skinless and boneless
    chicken breasts, cut into 2½-cm
    (1-in) cubes or cut into strips

Marinade

250 ml (9 fl oz) buttermilk

1 tbsp lemon juice

1 tsp soy sauce

1 tsp dried oregano

½ tsp paprika

1 garlic clove, peeled and sliced

Coating

2 x 150 g bags of flavoured crisps
    (e.g. Cheese and Onion or Roast
    Chicken crisps, or you could use
    two different flavours)

2 eggs

salt and pepper, to season

110 g (4 oz) plain flour

sunflower oil, for greasing

Tomato dip

6 tbsp tomato ketchup

1½ tsp sweet chilli sauce

2 tbsp lime juice

Maple mustard dip

8 tbsp mayonnaise

1½ tsp wholegrain mustard

1 tbsp maple syrup

2 tsp cold water

★ Mix together the buttermilk, lemon juice, soy sauce, oregano, paprika and garlic. Add the chicken, toss to coat, place in a covered bowl and marinate overnight in the fridge.

★ The next day, whiz the crisps to crumbs in a food processor or put them in a bag and crush using a rolling pin. Transfer the crumbs to a large bowl.

★ Whisk the eggs in a bowl with 1 tablespoon of water and a pinch of salt. In another bowl, mix the flour with a little black pepper.

★ Remove the chicken from the marinade, shaking off any excess. Working with 3 or 4 pieces of chicken at a time, dust the chicken with the flour, dip in the egg, then roll in the crisp crumbs to coat. Sit the coated chicken pieces on a tray or baking sheet lined with cling film.

★ Pre-heat the oven to 200°C/400°F/Gas 6. Transfer the nuggets to a lightly oiled baking sheet and bake for 15 minutes, turning over halfway through.

★ Whilst the nuggets are baking, whip up the dips by simply mixing the ingredients together in a bowl.

Party planning

Freeze the coated, uncooked nuggets up to 1 month in advance. Cover the baking sheet lined with cling film with more cling film and freeze the nuggets until solid. When frozen, transfer the nuggets to re-sealable bags. Bake them direct from frozen on a greased baking sheet, as above, adding 2–3 minutes to the cooking time.

sparkling ruby mocktail

To make sparkling emeralds, replace the cranberry juice with half blueberry and half pomegranate juice. This is delicious made using just sparkling water, but kids often prefer it sweeter and made with lemonade.

Makes 4 drinks (easily increased)
4 blueberries
4 raspberries
4 small mint leaves
400 ml (14 fl oz) cranberry juice, chilled
200 ml (7 fl oz) lemonade or sparkling
   water, chilled

★ Half-fill 12 holes in an ice-cube tray with water and put a blueberry, a raspberry, or a mint leaf in each one. Freeze for 3–4 hours, until solid, then top up with water and freeze overnight.
★ Mix the chilled juice and lemonade or sparkling water together in a large jug and pour into glasses. Drop in the ice cubes before serving.

jewelled couscous

Dried cranberries are the little gems in this warm couscous salad.

Makes 4 portions
170 g (6 oz) couscous
300 ml (½ pint) hot vegetable or
   chicken stock
30 g (1 oz) butter, melted
1 tsp lemon juice
salt and pepper, to season
55 g (2 oz) dried cranberries
4 spring onions, thinly sliced
1 tbsp chopped coriander (optional)

★ Put the couscous in a bowl and add the hot stock, butter and lemon juice. Cover and leave to stand for 5 minutes, until the liquid has been absorbed. Fluff with a fork and season to taste with salt and pepper. Stir in the cranberries, onions and coriander, if using, and serve warm.

ruby-glazed chicken

Jewel-toned pomegranate juice makes a sweet and sticky glaze for chicken – likely to tempt even the pickiest princess. Serve with the jewelled couscous (opposite).

Makes 4 portions
250 ml (9 fl oz) pomegranate juice
4 tbsp tomato ketchup
4 tbsp plum sauce
2 tsp soy sauce
4 chicken breasts, skin on and either
   on or off the bone

Party planning
Freeze the uncooked chicken in the marinade up to 1 month in advance. Defrost overnight in the fridge before cooking as above.

★ Put the pomegranate juice in a large bowl and whisk in the ketchup and the plum and soy sauces. Add the chicken, cover, and marinate overnight in the fridge.

★ Pre-heat the oven to 200°C/400°F/Gas 6. Put the chicken in a roasting tin and pour over the marinade. For chicken on the bone, cover the tin with foil and bake for 15 minutes. Uncover, baste the chicken with the juices in the tin and bake for a further 30 minutes, basting every 10 minutes. For boneless chicken, bake uncovered for 30 minutes, basting every 10 minutes with the juices in the tin.

★ Remove the chicken from the oven and allow to rest for 10 minutes before serving, as the glaze can be very hot. If your child prefers their meat off the bone, slice the chicken off before serving.

make-up
and jewellery

1 Bracelets

The little bracelets and ring were made by spraying some of the small star shaped/
flower-shaped pasta from my Baby Pasta range on some newspaper with spray glue
(spray mount) and coloured spray paints. You can also get beads with letters of the
alphabet to make bracelets with the children's names. These are all available at art
shops. ★ It's important to supervise the children when they make these as both are
quite toxic! Sprinkle the pasta shapes with glitter before they are completely dry
and just run them through your fingers so that they do not stick together. These
can be prepared in advance if you like. Have a collection of beads and sequins for
threading alternately on thin ribbon once the pasta shapes are dry, or you could
use elasticated thread.

2 Mirror invitations

You will need coloured card, shiny silver card or use foil, acrylic gems, glue and glitter glue. ★ Cut out hand-held mirror shapes from the coloured card and then cut out an oval shape from the silver card or foil and stick this in the centre. Write details of the party on the silver card or foil. Decorate the mirror with acrylic gems stuck on with glue and decorate with glitter glue.

3 Physalis (cape gooseberry) necklace

Simply tie about 15 physalis on a ribbon about 60 cm (24 in) long. Add orange bows at the front for decoration. To fasten, tie each end of the ribbon at the back.

4 Place cards

Make place cards with the children's names and a kiss of red lipstick. Or thread beads onto a ribbon to spell your guest's name.

5 Mini makeovers

Each little princess can have a mini makeover with washable sparkly make-up. Put together a dressing-up box with costumes, feather boas and fake jewellery. Take photos of everyone and send them afterwards.

'string of pearls'

Most pearl necklaces are fun to wear, but this one is nicer to eat, thanks to the pearls being mini meatballs on strings of spaghetti. The mixture of beef and pork or chicken keeps the meatballs light, but do use all beef if you prefer.

Makes 8 portions (easily halved)

Tomato sauce
2 tbsp olive oil
2 red onions, finely chopped
1 fat garlic clove, crushed
1 large carrot, peeled and grated
½ red pepper, diced
2 x 400 g cans chopped tomatoes
200 ml (7 fl oz) vegetable stock
4 tbsp tomato purée
2 tbsp sun-dried tomato paste
1 tbsp sugar
½ tsp dried oregano

Meatballs
100 g (3½ oz) fresh breadcrumbs
4 tbsp milk
1 apple, peeled and grated
4 tbsp grated Parmesan, plus extra to serve
1 tsp clear honey
1 egg yolk
1 tsp tomato puree
225 g (8 oz) minced beef
225 g (8 oz) minced pork or chicken
¼ tsp grated nutmeg, or to taste
salt and pepper, to season
flour, for dusting
sunflower oil, for frying
500 g (1 lb 2oz) spaghetti

★ First, make the tomato sauce. Heat the olive oil in a large saucepan and sauté the onions for 8–10 minutes, until soft. Stir in the garlic, then transfer half of the onions to a bowl and set aside.

★ Add the carrot and pepper to the saucepan and sauté for a further 4–5 minutes, until the vegetables are soft. Add the tomatoes, stock, tomato purée, sun-dried tomato paste, sugar and oregano, bring to the boil, then reduce the heat and simmer for 25–30 minutes, until thick.

★ Meanwhile, mix the breadcrumbs and milk with the reserved onions. Squeeze half the juice from the apple and add the grated apple to the breadcrumb mixture. Add the Parmesan, honey, egg yolk, tomato purée, beef and pork or chicken. Season to taste with the nutmeg and salt and pepper and mix together until thoroughly combined.

★ Form the meat mixture into 40 meatballs (using 1 heaped teaspoonful for each) and dust with flour. Heat a thin layer of sunflower oil in a large non-stick frying pan and brown the meatballs on all sides (you may need to do this in batches). Drain on kitchen paper.

★ Meanwhile, cook the spaghetti in a large pan of salted boiling water according to the packet instructions.

★ Purée the tomato sauce until smooth, and season to taste with salt and pepper. Add the meatballs, return to the heat and simmer for 5 minutes.

★ Drain the spaghetti and arrange in rings on plates. Spoon over the tomato sauce and sit the meatballs on the spaghetti 'ropes'. Serve with extra Parmesan.

Party planning
Cook the meatballs and sauce up to 1 month ahead and freeze. Defrost overnight in the fridge and reheat gently in a saucepan.

jewel jellies

Ruby-red raspberries and cranberry juice make delicious jewel-coloured jellies that every pretty princess will love.

Makes 8 portions (100 ml/
3½ fl oz each; easily halved)
340 g (12 oz) raspberries, fresh or frozen
110 g (4 oz) granulated sugar
750 ml (1¼ pints) cranberry juice
2 x 135 g blocks of raspberry or
    strawberry jelly
raspberries and blueberries, to decorate
yoghurt or whipped cream, to serve

Party planning
The jellies can be made up to 2 days ahead. Refrigerate until needed and decorate just before serving.

★ Put the raspberries, sugar and 300 ml (½ pint) of the juice in a pan over a medium heat. Heat gently, stirring frequently, until the sugar has dissolved, then bring to the boil and cook for 1 minute.

★ Remove from the heat and cool slightly, then sieve, pressing down on the pulp to extract as much juice as possible. Discard the pulp left behind in the sieve. Use the sieved juice (you should have approximately 400 ml/ 14 fl oz) to make up the jelly, following the packet instructions, then stir in the remaining cranberry juice.

★ Pour into glasses and refrigerate overnight to set. To serve, pile raspberries and blueberries on top of the jellies and hand them round with a bowl of yoghurt or whipped cream alongside.

jewelled cupcakes

Let your party girls create their own jewelled cupcakes, topped with a swirl of icing and a variety of 'gems'. (You can buy edible jewels at Squire's Kitchen; see page 158). You could use ready-made buttercream instead of the cream cheese icing, if you prefer.

Makes 10

125 g (4½ oz) butter or margarine
125 g (4½ oz) caster sugar
½ tsp lemon zest
2 eggs
125 g (4½ oz) self-raising flour
¼ tsp baking powder

Cream cheese icing
110 g (4 oz) cream cheese, at room
   temperature
110 g (4 oz) butter, at room temperature
½ tsp vanilla extract
85 g (3 oz) icing sugar
Edible food colouring

Decorations
edible jewels
jelly beans in bright colours
Jelly Tots
jelly diamonds
Smarties or M&Ms in bright colours
sugar diamonds

Party planning
The cakes can be made up to 1 month
in advance and frozen, un-iced, in a
plastic box. Defrost them at room
temperature for around 1 hour, and
then ice and decorate as above.

★ Pre-heat the oven to 180°C/350°F/Gas 4. Line a 12-hole muffin tin with 10 paper cases.

★ Cream the butter or margarine in an electric food mixer until soft. Add the sugar and beat until fluffy, then mix in the lemon zest. Add the eggs, one at a time. Add 1 tablespoon of the flour with the second egg, beating continuously. Sift over the remaining flour and baking powder then fold in gently. Divide the mixture between the paper cases and cook in the oven for about 20 minutes or until golden and springy to the touch.

★ Remove from the oven and cool in the muffin tin for 15 minutes, then transfer to a wire rack to cool completely.

★ Whilst the cupcakes are baking you can prepare the icing. Beat together the cream cheese and butter. Beat in the vanilla, then sift over the sugar and stir in until the sugar is combined. Beat for 1 minute until fluffy. Transfer to a bowl and set aside in the fridge. If you wish, you can divide the icing into two bowls and colour each with a few drops of the different food colourings.

★ Once the cakes are cold, swirl some of the icing on top of them and stick a selection of decorations into the icing. Leave to stand for around 30 minutes to allow the icing to set.

valentine's
day

cupid's arrows

Shoot these delicious arrows onto little princesses' plates and they will be swooning with delight.

Makes 8 skewers

340 g (12 oz) skinless, boneless chicken breasts, cut into approx. 2 cm (¾ in) cubes

2 red peppers

Marinade

2 tbsp natural yoghurt

100 ml (3½ fl oz) milk

1 tsp lemon juice

1 tsp fresh thyme leaves or ¼ tsp dried

¼ tsp mild paprika

1 garlic clove, crushed

¼ tsp salt

some freshly ground black pepper

Dip

4 tbsp tomato ketchup

4 tbsp mayonnaise

1 tsp sweet chilli sauce

½ tsp clear honey

You will also need 8 wooden skewers, soaked in water for at least 30 minutes

★ Whisk the marinade ingredients together in a bowl along with a good grinding of black pepper. Add the chicken and stir to coat, then cover and marinate overnight in the fridge.

★ Cut each pepper into quarters and remove the seeds. Cut out heart shapes using mini-cutters or cut into triangles to act as the arrowhead. Put them on a plate, cover with cling film and chill until needed. Stir together the ingredients for the dip, cover and chill until needed.

★ Pre-heat the grill to high. Thread the chicken on to the skewers, leaving a space at the top of each skewer. Season the chicken with a little salt and pepper and grill for 4–5 minutes, until half cooked. Turn the skewers over and thread a red pepper heart or triangle on to the top of each skewer. Grill for a further 4–5 minutes, until the chicken is cooked through and the pepper is soft.

★ Transfer the dip to small bowls and serve with the skewers.

rice krispie hearts

These fun lollipops will be loved by many little princesses – and probably a few princes, too. I used a Wilton's heart-shaped cookie pan (they call it a Cookie Treat Pan; see page 158), with which you can make 6 individual heart-shaped lollipops.

**Makes 6 hearts
(or 8–10 in a thinner pan)**
55 g (2 oz) butter
1 tbsp golden syrup
a pinch of salt
150 g (5½ oz) white chocolate, chopped
2–3 drops red or pink food colouring
   (optional, but it gives it a nice
   pink colour)
55 g (2 oz) Rice Krispies
red writing icing
wooden skewers or lollipop sticks

Party planning
The hearts can be made up to 2 days ahead and stored in an airtight container in the fridge. Ice the hearts and insert the sticks just before serving, if adding the sticks when cooked and cooled.

★ Put the butter, syrup and salt in a fairly large saucepan, and put the chocolate in a large bowl. Heat the butter and syrup until the butter has melted, then stir in the red food colouring, if using. Pour the warm butter and syrup over the chocolate and stir until the chocolate has melted. Alternatively, stir the chocolate into the butter and syrup mixture (off the heat) until melted.

★ Add the Rice Krispies and stir until they are well coated in the chocolate. Press the mixture into a heart-shaped cookie pan, push in the wooden skewers or lollipop sticks and chill until solid (about 2 hours). Remove from the moulds by levering gently with a blunt knife.

★ If you don't have a heart-shaped pan, line the base of a 20 x 20 cm (8 x 8 in) cake tin with baking parchment and press the Rice Krispies and chocolate mixture into the tin. Chill until just firm (about 30 minutes) then cut out hearts using a lightly oiled 6 cm (2½in) heart-shaped cookie cutter. Transfer the hearts to a baking sheet and chill until solid, then insert a wooden skewer or lollipop stick into each to make a lollipop.

★ Decorate the hearts using the writing icing and store them in a cool place, or the fridge.

pizza hearts

Perfect for princesses with a passion for pizza!

**Makes 8 hearts (4 portions
as a main course, 8 portions
as part of a party table)**

Sauce

1 tbsp olive oil

1 small onion, chopped

¼ red pepper, approx. 45 g (1½ oz),
diced

1 small carrot, approx. 50 g (1¾ oz),
peeled and grated

1 garlic clove, crushed

1 x 400 g can chopped tomatoes

1 tbsp tomato purée

1 tbsp sun-dried tomato purée

1 tsp sugar

salt and pepper, to season

4 muffins, split in half, or 2 x 20 cm (8 in)
ready-made (part-baked) pizza bases

140 g (5 oz) grated mozzarella or
Cheddar

*You will also need a 6–7 cm (2½–3 in)
heart-shaped cookie cutter*

Party planning
The sauce can be made up to
1 month in advance and frozen.
Defrost overnight in the fridge.

★ To make the sauce, heat the oil in a wok or large frying pan and sauté the onion, pepper and carrot for 8–10 minutes, until soft. Add the garlic and cook for 1 minute more. Add the remaining sauce ingredients, bring to the boil, then reduce the heat and simmer for 20–25 minutes until thick. Season to taste with salt and pepper, then blend the sauce until smooth.

★ Pre-heat the oven to 200°C/400°F/Gas 6. Cut 8 hearts out of the muffin halves or pizza bases using a 6–7 cm (2½–3 in) cutter. Put the hearts on a baking sheet and spread ½ tablespoon of tomato sauce over each heart, then top each one with a little cheese. Bake for 9–10 minutes, until the bases are crisp and the cheese is bubbling. If the cheese melts over the sides of the pizzas it can be nudged back into shape with the tip of a table knife. Cool slightly before serving.

★ There will be some tomato sauce left over – this can be frozen and used for pizzas on another day, or tossed into hot pasta.

valentine's day

1 Snapdragons

Cut out a square about 20 cm (8 in) square. Fold in the corners so that they meet in the middle. Flip it over, then fold in the corners again. You will have 8 triangles: write the numbers from 1 to 8 on each triangle, lift up and write a message or a forfeit under triangle, then fold the two sides together to form a rectangle. Draw designs on each square. To play, put your thumbs and forefingers into the pockets. Ask your partner for a number. Open and shut the snapdragon the required number of times – then ask your partner to choose one of the numbers. Open that number and read out the message, e.g. Tell me a secret, Sing me a song, Do a somersault etc.

2 Rice krispie hearts

Why not make individual lollipops in the shape of hearts (see page 26)?

3 Glitter glasses
Brush the inside of a tumbler with honey, sprinkle some coloured sugar into the glass and swirl it around so that it sticks to the inside of the glass. When you pour passion potion (see page 30) into the glass the sugar will dissolve.

4 Party invitations
Write the details of a party on a small piece of paper, then roll it up, tie with a red ribbon and place in a pink heart-shaped box. Sprinkle with glittery mini-hearts.

5 Valentine's make-and-do
Everyone can make their own Valentine's cards, cut out and decorate paper hearts or decorate heart-shaped boxes with glitter, ribbons and pink pom-poms.

passion potion

If you can't get fresh berries, frozen work just as well. The berries can be a bit tart at this time of year, so do taste the drink and add extra sugar if needed.

Makes 4 portions served in 200 ml (7 fl oz) glasses (easily doubled)
225 g (8 oz) raspberries, fresh or frozen
300 g (11 oz) strawberries, fresh or frozen
55 g (2 oz) sugar, add extra to taste (optional)
400 ml (14 fl oz) sparkling or still apple juice, well chilled

★ If using frozen fruit, leave it to stand at room temperature for 20–30 minutes first to allow it to soften slightly. Put the berries and sugar into a blender and liquidize. Taste and add more sugar if necessary. Sieve the purée to remove the seeds – you should have around 400 ml (14 fl oz). You can make this a day in advance and chill until needed.

★ Transfer the purée to a large jug and stir in the apple juice. Serve in tall glasses or champagne flutes.

chocolate fondue

A delicious dip for your princess to share with her favourite friends.

Makes 4 portions (easily doubled)
Fondue
55 g (2 oz) plain chocolate, chopped
55 g (2 oz) milk chocolate, chopped
50 ml (2 fl oz) double cream
1 tbsp golden syrup
¼ tsp vanilla extract
To dip, a selection of:
fresh fruit (e.g. strawberries, seedless grapes, mango chunks, banana slices, apple wedges), mini meringues, plain biscuits or cookies, plain Madeira cake, cut into cubes

★ Put the chocolate, cream, syrup and vanilla extract into a medium heatproof bowl. Put the bowl over, but not in, a saucepan of warm water and melt the chocolate, stirring occasionally. The chocolate can also be melted in a microwave in 2 or 3 bursts of 15 seconds each, stirring between each burst.

★ Remove the bowl from the saucepan and serve the fondue immediately, dipping the fruit, mini meringues, biscuits, cookies and cake into the melted chocolate. Hand out forks or skewers for spearing some of the more slippery fruits.

passion pink pasta

A perfectly pink sauce to please pasta-loving princesses. This is one of my favourite tomato sauces for pasta. The trick to making a creamy tomato sauce is to have quite an intense tomato base, which is why I have put in so many tomato flavourings. Serve with or without the smoked salmon.

Makes 8 portions

1 tbsp olive oil
1 small red onion, chopped
1 garlic clove, crushed
1 tsp balsamic vinegar
2 x 400 g cans chopped tomatoes
30 g (1 oz) SunBlush tomatoes
2 tbsp tomato purée
2 tbsp sun-dried tomato purée
2 tbsp tomato ketchup
2 tsp sugar
500 g (1 lb 2oz) pasta shapes (hearts are fun, otherwise penne are good)
150 ml (5½ fl oz) double cream
salt and pepper, to season
a small handful of basil leaves (shredded if large)
110 g (4 oz) smoked salmon, cut into thin strips (optional)
grated Parmesan, to serve

Party planning

The tomato base can be made up to 1 month ahead and frozen. Defrost overnight in the fridge and warm gently in a saucepan before adding the cream.

★ Heat the oil in a wok or large saucepan and sauté the onion for 7–8 minutes, until soft. Add the garlic and balsamic vinegar and cook for 1–2 minutes, until the vinegar has evaporated. Transfer to a blender and add all of the tomato ingredients, then blend until smooth.

★ Return the tomato sauce to the wok or pan and add the sugar. Bring to the boil then reduce the heat and simmer for 30–40 minutes, until thick and reduced by about half. Meanwhile, cook the pasta in lightly salted boiling water according to the packet instructions. Reserve a teacupful of the pasta cooking water when draining the pasta.

★ Add the cream to the sauce and season to taste with salt and pepper. Add the drained pasta and toss to coat, adding a little of the pasta cooking water, 1 tablespoon at a time, if the sauce becomes too thick.

★ Spoon the pasta onto warmed plates and scatter over the basil and smoked salmon, if using. Serve with the grated Parmesan.

shortbread sweethearts

A very delicious way to say I ♡ you.

Makes 8 (easily doubled)

Shortbread

55 g (2 oz) butter, softened

30 g (1 oz) caster sugar

¼ tsp vanilla extract

a pinch of salt

85 g (3 oz) plain flour, plus extra
   for rolling

To sandwich the hearts

40 g (1½ oz) white chocolate, chopped

icing sugar, for dusting

approx. 1 tbsp raspberry jam
   (preferably seedless)

*You will also need 2 heart-shaped
cookie cutters, one 6 cm (2½ in) and
the other a little smaller*

Party planning

The shortbread dough can be cut
out and frozen on baking sheets
lined with baking parchment. Transfer
to a re-sealable box once solid and
bake direct from frozen, as described
above. The baked and sandwiched
shortbreads can be stored in an
airtight container in a cool place for
up to 24 hours. Chilling the dough in
the freezer or fridge before cooking
helps keep the shortbread in shape
when it is baked in the oven.

★ Beat the butter, sugar, vanilla and a pinch of salt until combined. Add the flour and stir in with a wooden spoon, then bring the dough together with your hands. If the dough is very soft, wrap in cling film and chill for around 30 minutes.

★ Roll the shortbread dough out on a lightly floured surface to around 2 mm (¹/₁₆ in) thick. Cut out 16 heart shapes using a 6 cm (2½ in) cookie cutter, re-rolling the scraps as necessary. Put 8 dough hearts on one lightly greased baking sheet. Cut out heart centres from the remaining 8 dough hearts, using a small heart-shaped cookie cutter. Transfer the shortbread with the hearts cut out to a second lightly greased baking sheet. Chill both baking sheets for 10 minutes in the freezer or 1 hour in the fridge.

★ Pre-heat the oven to 180°C/350°F/Gas 4. Bake the shortbread until slightly golden around the edges – this will take about 10–12 minutes for the ones with hearts cut out of the centre and 13–15 minutes for the solid ones. Cool on the baking sheets for 5 minutes then transfer to a wire rack to cool completely.

★ Melt the white chocolate in a small heatproof bowl set over, not in, a pan of warm water. Stir frequently and watch it carefully, as white chocolate can overheat very easily. Remove the bowl from the pan when you can still see a few un-melted lumps of chocolate and stir the mixture until smooth. Set aside for 10–20 minutes to let the chocolate cool and thicken slightly. Meanwhile, dust the cookies with the cut-out centres with icing sugar.

★ When cool, spread a scant ½ tablespoon of white chocolate over each solid heart cookie, leaving a border around the edge (the chocolate will spread as you sandwich the cookies). Put a blob of jam, about ¼ teaspoon, in the centre of each. Sandwich the cookies with the sugar-dusted tops (hold by the edges to avoid fingerprints in the icing sugar) and add a little extra jam in the cut-out centre, if needed. Chill for 10–20 minutes, until the chocolate has set, then store in a cool place.

little red velvet cakes

Little princesses love to give gifts, and what could be more perfect than mini heart-shaped red velvet cakes?

Makes 4 cakes (each cake serves 3–4)

Cake

150 g (5½ oz) plain flour
1 tbsp cocoa powder
1 tsp baking powder
⅛ tsp bicarbonate of soda
¼ tsp salt
150 ml (¼ pint) milk
2 tsp red food colouring
85 g (3 oz) butter, softened,
    plus extra for greasing
150 g (5½ oz) caster sugar
1 egg, plus 2 yolks
1½ tsp vanilla extract

Icing

200 g (7 oz) cream cheese, at room
    temperature
150 g (5½ oz) butter, at room
    temperature
150 g (5½ oz) icing sugar
½ tsp vanilla extract

red and pink candy-coated chocolate or
sprinkles, and edible flowers, to decorate
(www.cybercandy.co.uk sells dark and
light pink, white and red M&Ms)

Party planning

The cake can be baked and frozen, un-iced, wrapped in cling film and foil, up to 1 month in advance. Defrost for 2–3 hours at room temperature, then cut and ice as above.

★ Grease and line the base of 4 individual, springform, heart-shaped cake tins, about 10 cm (4 in) wide and 4 cm (2 in) deep. If you don't have individual heart-shaped tins, you could make this in one large heart-shaped tin that is 20 cm (8 in) across. You can also buy cupcake trays with the cupcakes shaped like little hearts. Pre-heat the oven to 180°C/350°F/Gas 4.

★ Sift together the flour, cocoa, baking powder, bicarbonate of soda and salt. Heat the milk in a saucepan or microwave until lukewarm, add the food colouring and set aside.

★ Cream the butter and sugar until pale and fluffy. Beat together the egg, yolks and vanilla and beat into the butter, a little at a time. Mix in a third of the flour, then half of the coloured milk, a third of the flour, the rest of the milk and finally the remaining flour.

★ Spoon the batter into the prepared tin(s) and spread out evenly. Tap the base of the cake tin(s) on a work surface 2–3 times to level the batter, then bake for 20–25 minutes until the cakes are risen, firm to the touch and a skewer comes out clean when inserted into the centre. (One large cake will take 25–30 minutes.) Leave the cake(s) to cool in the tins for 30 minutes, then invert onto a cooling rack, peel away the paper and leave the cake(s) to cool completely.

★ Meanwhile, make the icing by beating together the cream cheese and butter until smooth (this is much easier to do if the cream cheese and butter are at the same temperature). Beat in the icing sugar and vanilla. If the icing is very soft, refrigerate for 15–20 minutes to firm up.

★ Split the cake(s) in half horizontally. Spread a quarter of the icing over the base(s) and sandwich the hearts back together. Ice the tops with the remaining icing. Decorate the tops with red and pink sweets or sprinkles and/or edible flowers. Store the cake(s) in a cool place, preferably in airtight containers. The iced cake(s) will keep in a cool place for 1–2 days.

★ If making the cakes as gifts it may be helpful to place each one on a large piece of baking parchment or foil before icing. The paper can then be used to lift the cakes in and out of boxes.

easter
princess

egg head sandwiches

For added fun, cut these sandwiches into shapes using a cookie cutter and decorate in any way you like.

Makes 4 open sandwiches (easily increased)
7 eggs
4–5 tbsp mayonnaise
salt and freshly ground black pepper
4 slices bread, buttered
Decoration
sliced red pepper, grated carrot,
    olives, salami, gherkins, chives,
    basil, peas, cherry tomatoes

★ Bring a saucepan of water to the boil and gently lower in the eggs. Simmer the eggs for 12 minutes then carefully drain off the boiling water. Fill the saucepan with cold water and leave the eggs inside until cool. (The eggs can be boiled up to 2 days ahead and stored, unpeeled, in the fridge.)
★ Peel the eggs and slice 2 using an egg slicer or a knife. Set aside 8 of the slices to make the eyes. Place the remaining pieces in a bowl with the remaining 5 eggs. Mash with a fork and add the mayonnaise. Season to taste.
★ Cover all 4 slices of bread with egg mayonnaise. Make the faces using the toppings shown in the photo as inspiration.

cheese soufflés

Cheese soufflés as light as a spring breeze.

Makes 6 soufflés (can be halved)
55 g (2 oz) butter, plus extra
    for greasing
85 g (3 oz) grated Parmesan
30 g (1 oz) plain flour
240 ml (8½ fl oz) milk
55 g (2 oz) Cheddar, grated
55 g (2 oz) Gruyère, grated
4 eggs, separated
paprika, to season
grated nutmeg, to season
salt and pepper, to season

★ Pre-heat the oven to 200°C/400°F/Gas 6 with a baking sheet inside. Grease 6 large ramekins and dust the insides with 2 tablespoons of the grated Parmesan.
★ Melt the butter and stir in the flour. Whisk in the milk and cook, whisking constantly, until the sauce thickens and comes to the boil. Remove from the heat and cool slightly, then stir in the three cheeses until melted. Stir in the egg yolks and season generously with paprika, nutmeg, salt and pepper (the mixture will be much less strong when the egg whites are incorporated).
★ Put the egg whites plus a pinch of salt into a clean bowl and whisk to floppy peaks. Stir a quarter of the whites into the cheese sauce, then fold in the remainder.
★ Spoon the mixture into the prepared ramekins and bake in the oven on the pre-heated baking sheet for 16–18 minutes until risen and golden.
★ Serve immediately.

easter simnel cake

A Simnel cake is a light fruit cake, similar to a Christmas cake, that is covered in marzipan. A layer of marzipan or almond paste is also baked into the middle of the cake. On the top of the cake, around the edge, are eleven marzipan balls; these represent the true apostles of Jesus (Judas is omitted). In some variations, Christ is also represented by a ball placed in the centre. Your princess can help to measure and mix all the cake ingredients and she will enjoy rolling the marzipan into little balls.

Serves 10 or more
200 g (7 oz) caster sugar
200 g (7 oz) butter, softened
250 g (9 oz) self-raising flour
4 large eggs
zest of 1 orange
1 tbsp mixed spice
250 g (9 oz) sultanas
150 g (5 oz) ready-to-eat dried apricots,
    chopped into small pieces
50 g (2 oz) stem ginger, finely chopped
Topping
2 tbsp apricot jam
450 g (1 lb) golden marzipan
fresh flowers or icing flowers,
    to decorate

★ Pre-heat the oven to 150°C/300°F/Gas 2. Base-line and grease a 23 cm (9 in) round springform tin.

★ Mix the caster sugar, butter, flour, eggs, orange zest and mixed spice together in a mixing bowl until smooth. Add the prepared fruit and mix well. Spoon half of the cake mixture into the base of the tin. Roll one third of the marzipan out into a 23 cm (9 in) circle and place on top of the cake mixture. Spoon the remaining cake mixture on top and level.

★ Bake in the oven for about 1¾–2 hours or until golden brown and firm to the touch. Remove from the tin and leave to cool completely.

★ Meanwhile, roll another third of the marzipan out to a 23 cm (9 in) circle. When the cake is cold, melt the jam in a small pan, then brush it over the top of the cake and place the marzipan circle on top. Divide the remaining third of the marzipan into 11 pieces and shape into little balls by rolling them between your palms. Position these around the edge of the cake. Arrange fresh flowers or flowers made of icing in the middle of the cake to finish off the decoration.

easter princess

1 Easter biscuits
Roll out ginger biscuit dough, cut out little rabbit, chick and duck shapes and when baked, decorate with icing and silver balls (see page 48).

2 Party invitations
Make egg-shaped invitations from card and thread a piece of string and a bead through the top.

3 Egg place names

Hard-boil some eggs and decorate them with paint and stickers, or use as a place setting in a small basket with the child's name written on.

4 Butterfly straws

Make butterfly wing straws by cutting fancy paper into butterfly shapes and making two slits through which you can thread a couple of straws.

5 Egg people

Decorate hard-boiled eggs. Make hats from egg cartons, empty toilet rolls and odds and ends like feathers, lace and ribbon. You can make plaits from wool and paint faces on the eggs with felt-tip pens.

hot cross bunnies

Your cute and cuddly bunnies will love to nibble on these hot cross bunnies for breakfast.

Makes 8 large or 12 medium buns

Bunnies

150 ml (5½ fl oz) milk
100 ml (3½ fl oz) cold water
450 g (1 lb) strong white flour,
 plus extra for kneading
1 x 7 g sachet easy-blend yeast
50 g (2 oz) soft light brown sugar
1 tbsp ground mixed spice
1 tsp salt
50 g (2 oz) butter, melted
1 egg, beaten
sunflower oil, for greasing
110 g (4 oz) raisins
30 g (1 oz) mixed peel

Decoration

2 tbsp milk
2 tbsp caster sugar
24 or 36 currants (you need 3 per bunny)

Party planning

Mix the bread dough and allow it to rise, then form into the ovals on a baking sheet lined with cling film. Cover with a layer of cling film and freeze until solid. Transfer to re-sealable bags and freeze for up to 1 month. To defrost, put the frozen rolls on greased baking sheets, cover with a clean, damp tea towel and leave in a warm place to defrost and prove for 3–4 hours. Then continue as above.

★ Put the milk in a saucepan and bring to the boil. Immediately remove from the heat and add the water, then leave to cool for 5 minutes.

★ Put the flour in a large bowl and stir in the yeast, sugar, mixed spice and salt until well blended. Make a dent in the centre and add the butter and egg, then add the milk and water mixture and combine to make a soft dough, adding a little extra water if needed.

★ Knead the dough on a lightly floured surface for about 10 minutes, until smooth and elastic. Put in a large oiled bowl and cover with cling film. Leave to rise in a warm place for 1½–2 hours, or until doubled in size.

★ Turn out the dough onto a lightly floured surface and pat into a large round. Scatter the raisins and mixed peel over the dough, fold it in half and half again, then knead the dough to incorporate the fruit.

★ Divide the dough into 8 or 12 equal portions. Roll each portion of dough into a ball and put them all on 2 greased baking sheets, spaced well apart. Press the dough balls down slightly and shape the ends so that they are oval-shaped rather than round.

★ Cover with a clean, damp tea towel and leave to rise for 30–45 minutes until almost doubled in size.

★ Meanwhile, pre-heat the oven to 200°C/400°F/Gas 6.

★ To make the bunny ears, use kitchen scissors to make 2 long cuts at one end of each ball. You need to hold the scissors fairly flat against the top of the rolls, scissor points facing towards the end of the dough ball. Make 2 cuts side by side and slightly pull up the cut dough to form ears. Form a tail by making a small downwards snip at the other end, where the rabbit's rump would be, or you could make a bobtail by adding a small ball of dough. Bake the buns for 15 minutes.

★ Meanwhile, make the glaze by heating the milk and sugar in a small saucepan until the sugar has dissolved. Remove the buns from the oven and reduce the heat to 180°C/350°F/Gas 4. Brush the milk and sugar glaze all over the buns and stick 3 currants on each face end to make eyes and a nose. Return the buns to the oven and bake for a further 5 minutes for the smaller rolls and 7–8 minutes for the larger rolls. Transfer to a wire rack to cool.

little lamb burgers with cucumber-mint sauce

Seasonal Easter lamb can be turned into tasty little burgers and served with a fresh yoghurt sauce. I think lamb is much nicer grilled, so I like to cook these that way. The olives disappear into the mixture so kids shouldn't see them, but you can omit them if you prefer.

Makes 8 small burgers (easily halved)

1 tbsp olive oil

1 medium red onion, finely chopped

1 garlic clove, crushed

45 g (1½ oz) pitted black olives

1 tbsp sun-dried tomato purée

½ tsp chopped fresh oregano
    or ¼ tsp dried

450 g (1 lb) minced lamb

2 tsp runny honey

1 tsp lemon juice

6–8 drops Tabasco (optional)

salt and pepper, to season

Sauce

½ cucumber, peeled, halved
    and seeded

8 large mint leaves, chopped

120 ml (4½ fl oz) Greek yoghurt

1 tsp lemon juice

To serve

pitta breads or burger buns,
    split in half

4 leaves iceberg lettuce, shredded

★ Heat the oil in a frying pan and sauté the onion for 6–8 minutes until soft. Add the garlic and cook for 1 minute more, then transfer to a food processor and add the olives, tomato purée and oregano. Whiz until everything is finely chopped, then add the lamb, honey, lemon juice and Tabasco, if using, and season to taste with salt and pepper. Pulse 4–5 times to combine, then divide the meat mixture into 8 and form into small burgers. Chill, covered, until needed.

★ To make the sauce, grate the cucumber and place it on a clean tea towel. Bring the corners of the tea towel together and twist until tight, then squeeze out as much water as possible. Transfer to a bowl and mix in the remaining sauce ingredients plus a pinch of salt.

★ Pre-heat the grill to high and cook the burgers for around 4 minutes each side, until brown and cooked through. Toast the pittas or burger buns and sit some lettuce inside the pitta or on the base of the bun. Add a lamb burger and top with sauce and the burger bun lid, if using.

Party planning

The burgers and sauce can be made a day in advance and stored in the fridge, covered, until needed. The burgers can also be made up to 1 month in advance and frozen: put the formed burgers on a baking sheet lined with cling film, cover with more cling film, freeze until solid then transfer to a plastic box. To defrost, sit the burgers on a baking sheet lined with cling film, cover and leave overnight in the fridge.

mini mimosa

Little bunnies love to sip on fresh and fruity cocktails, but adults may like to top their own glasses up with real fizz.

Makes 4 drinks (easily increased)
2 ripe passion fruits
2 tbsp icing sugar
400 ml (14 fl oz) fresh orange juice
200 ml (7 fl oz) sparkling lemonade

★ Halve the passion fruits and scoop the seeds and pulp into a bowl. Stir in the icing sugar until dissolved, then push the pulp through a sieve to extract the juice. Discard the black seeds.
★ Pour the orange juice into a jug and stir in the passion fruit juice. Top up with the lemonade and pour into champagne flutes to serve.

baby bunny muffin bites

Even the fussiest little rabbit will enjoy carrots in these mini muffins.

Makes approx. 18 (easily doubled)
55 g (2 oz) plain flour
¼ tsp baking powder
⅛ tsp bicarbonate of soda
¼ tsp mixed spice
½ tsp ground cinnamon
a large pinch of salt
55 g (2 oz) butter, melted
30 g (1 oz) soft light brown sugar
1 tbsp maple syrup
1 egg yolk
¼ tsp vanilla extract
50 g (2 oz) peeled and grated carrot
30 g (1 oz) raisins
Icing
30 g (1 oz) cream cheese
15 g (½ oz) butter
30 g (1 oz) dulche de leche
2 tbsp icing sugar

★ Pre-heat the oven to 180°C/350°F/Gas 4. Line a 24-hole mini-muffin tin with 18 paper cases.
★ Put all of the ingredients except the raisins in a food processor and whiz for 1 minute until well combined. Add the raisins and pulse 2–3 times.
★ Divide the batter between the paper cases, filling each one two-thirds full (approximately 2 teaspoons of batter per muffin). Bake for 12–14 minutes until risen and firm to the touch. Remove from the oven and leave to cool slightly, then transfer to a wire rack and leave to cool completely.
★ To make the icing, beat the cream cheese, butter and dulche de leche together and then beat in the icing sugar. Swirl a little icing on top of each muffin.

Party planning
The baked muffins can be frozen, un-iced, in plastic boxes or resealable bags for up to 1 month. Defrost for 1–2 hours at room temperature before icing.

bunny biscuits

These delicious, slightly chewy, ginger biscuits are great fun to make, as your little princess will enjoy rolling out dough and cutting it into shapes using cookie cutters.

Makes about 18 cookies
60 g (2 ½ oz) butter
50 g (1½ oz) soft brown sugar
4 tbsp golden syrup
150 g (5½ oz) plain flour, sieved,
　　plus extra for dusting
1 egg yolk
1 tsp ground ginger
½ tsp bicarbonate of soda
Decoration
2 tbsp apricot jam
coloured sugar sprinkles
　　or desiccated coconut
silver balls
sugar flowers
white writing icing
mini marshmallows

★ Pre-heat the oven to 180°C/350°F/Gas 4.

★ Beat the butter and sugar with an electric whisk until pale. Add the golden syrup, flour, egg yolk, ginger and bicarbonate of soda and beat together until it forms a dough. Wrap in cling film and chill for at least 30 minutes.

★ Roll out on a floured work surface to a thickness of about 3 mm (⅛ in). Start in the centre of the dough and roll evenly outwards. Cut into shapes using rabbit shaped or chick-shaped cookie cutters, working from the outside edges of the dough into the centre, cutting as close together as possible. Re-roll the trimmings until all the dough is used up.

★ Place the cookies on baking sheets lined with baking parchment and bake for about 9 minutes. Allow to cool slightly, then transfer to a wire rack to cool completely.

★ Once cool, warm the apricot jam in a small pan or in a bowl in the microwave until runny, and sieve. Brush a little jam in the centre of each biscuit and scatter over some sugar sprinkles or desiccated coconut. Use silver balls for eyes and noses and attach the sugar flowers with a blob of the writing icing. Do the same with a mini marshmallow for the bunny's tail.

chocolate nest cupcakes

Spring has sprung and nests are full of eggs – in this case, yummy chocolate ones.

Makes 10 cupcakes
30 g (1 oz) good-quality cocoa powder
120 ml (4½ fl oz) boiling water
(from a kettle)
55 g (2 oz) butter, at room temperature
100 g (3½ oz) caster sugar
1 egg
1 tsp vanilla extract
85 g (3 oz) self-raising flour
¼ tsp salt

Icing and decoration
55 g (2 oz) plain chocolate,
chopped or chips
110 g (4 oz) butter, at room temperature
110 g (4 oz) icing sugar
roughly crumbled Cadbury's Chocolate
Flake
30 mini chocolate eggs
(e.g. Cadbury's Mini Eggs)
10 mini chicks (optional, remove
before eating)

Party planning
The cupcakes can be made up to 1
month in advance and frozen, un-iced,
in plastic boxes. Defrost for about 2
hours at room temperature. The icing
can be made 1 week in advance and
kept in the fridge. Bring it to room
temperature before using.

★ Pre-heat the oven to 180°C/350°F/Gas 4. Line a 12-hole muffin tin with 10 paper cases.

★ Put the cocoa in a heatproof jug and add the boiling water. Stir until all of the cocoa has dissolved, then leave to cool. Cream the butter and sugar until pale and fluffy. Beat in the egg and the vanilla then trickle in the cooled cocoa, beating constantly. Sift over the flour and salt and fold in.

★ Divide the batter between the paper cases (they should be half-full) and bake for 15–17 minutes, until risen and firm to the touch. Remove from the oven and cool in the tin for 15 minutes, then carefully transfer the cupcakes to a wire rack to cool completely.

★ To make the icing, put the chocolate in a heatproof bowl set over, but not in, a saucepan of hot water. Stir occasionally until melted and smooth, then remove the bowl from the pan and leave the chocolate to cool slightly. The chocolate can also be melted in a microwave, in 2 or 3 bursts of 15 seconds each, stirring between each burst, until the chocolate has just melted.

★ Beat the butter until pale then beat in the cooled chocolate. Beat in the icing sugar, a little at a time, until you have a thick icing. If the icing is very soft, chill it for 30 minutes.

★ Using a palette knife, spread the icing over the tops of the cupcakes. Arrange the pieces of Chocolate Flake around the edges of the cakes to make the nest.

★ Sit 3 chocolate eggs in the centre of each nest and add a chick, if using.

movie star
sleepover

cinema-style nachos

Nachos are a popular snack now at the cinema – these home-made ones are tastier and much more healthy. As a bonus you can add extra yummy toppings; there are some suggested below, or you can add your own favourites. I used a combination of Red Leicester and mozzarella to mimic the stringy orange sauce that they serve with nachos in the cinema. If you prefer, you can use one kind of cheese.

Makes 4 portions

150 g (5½ oz) tortilla chips
   (approx. 4 large handfuls)
55 g (2 oz) grated Red Leicester cheese
55 g (2 oz) grated mozzarella
   (not the fresh type in water)
20 g (¾ oz) grated Parmesan

Salsa

300 g (10½ oz) cherry tomatoes
4 spring onions, roughly chopped
¼ red pepper
¼ fresh red chilli (optional)
salt and pepper, to season

Toppings

8 black olives, sliced
110 g (4 oz) mushrooms, thinly sliced
   and sautéed in 1 tbsp olive oil
6 slices salami, chopped
4 tbsp drained tinned sweetcorn

To serve (optional)

approx. 100 g (3½ oz) guacamole
approx. 4 tbsp soured cream

★ First, make the salsa. Halve the cherry tomatoes and squeeze out as many pips as possible. Put the tomatoes in a food processor with the spring onions, pepper and chilli, if using. Season to taste with salt and pepper and whiz for about 30 seconds to finely chop (but not purée) the ingredients. Scrape out into a sieve and leave to drain over a bowl for 10 minutes.

★ Pre-heat the grill to high and line a baking sheet with foil (or make 4 small foil trays, for individual portions). Spread out the tortilla chips in a single layer and spoon the salsa over. Mix the cheeses together. Scatter any (or all) of the toppings over the tortilla chips then top with the cheese.

★ Grill for 2–3 minutes, until the cheese has melted. Slide the foil onto a large plate or board and serve immediately with guacamole and soured cream, if liked.

Party planning

Make the salsa 1 day ahead. Store, covered, in the fridge until needed and stir before using.

star sandwiches

Dainty star-shaped sandwiches with deluxe fillings – perfect for a movie première party!

smoked salmon and cream cheese

Makes 4 sandwiches
4 slices white or brown bread
30 g (1 oz) butter, slightly softened
55 g (2 oz) cream cheese, slightly softened
2 large slices smoked salmon (approx. 55 g/2 oz)
a squeeze of lemon juice
black pepper, to season

You will need a 5–6 cm (2–2½ in) diameter star-shaped cutter to make star-shaped sandwiches

★ With a rolling pin, roll all the slices of bread to about half of their original thickness, then butter each one lightly with the softened butter. Spread the cream cheese over 2 of the slices and top with the smoked salmon. Sprinkle over a couple of drops of lemon juice and season to taste with black pepper. Top with the second slice of bread and cut out 2 star shapes from each sandwich.

Party planning
The sandwiches can be made up to 4 hours ahead, put on a plate and covered tightly with cling film. Store in the fridge until needed.

prawn cocktail

2 tbsp mayonnaise
1 tbsp tomato ketchup
½ tsp lemon juice
1–2 drops Tabasco (optional)
salt and pepper, to season
110 g (4 oz) small cooked prawns
4 slices white or brown bread, lightly buttered
a handful of cress or alfalfa

★ Mix together the mayonnaise, ketchup, lemon juice and Tabasco, if using. Season to taste with salt and pepper and stir in the prawns.
★ Divide the prawn mixture between 2 slices of the bread and spread out to the edges. Scatter over the cress or alfalfa and sandwich with the second slice of bread. Cut out 2 star shapes from each sandwich.
★ Other fillings to try – Egg and Chive (page 38), Chicken, Sweetcorn and Mayo (page 93), Ham and Cream Cheese (page 93).

Party planning
The prawn mixture can be made the day before and stored, covered, in the fridge overnight. Stir before using. The sandwiches can be made an hour ahead and kept in the fridge until needed.

sweet and sticky chicken drumettes

Sweet and sticky chicken is delicious to nibble while watching your favourite movie. The drumette is the meatiest part of the wing and looks a little like a miniature drumstick. If you can't get drumettes, use 8 wings instead; cut off and discard the wing tips then cut the remaining part of the wing in half at the joint. This is a great favourite with my two princesses!

Makes 16 drumettes or 8 portions (easily halved)

4 tbsp balsamic vinegar
4 tbsp clear honey
45 g (1½ oz) soft light brown sugar
1 tbsp tomato ketchup
16 chicken drumettes
salt and pepper, to season
2 tbsp toasted sesame seeds (optional)

★ Whisk the balsamic vinegar, honey, sugar and ketchup together. Put the drumettes in a large re-sealable bag and pour over the marinade. Expel as much air as possible from the bag then seal tightly and put in a bowl. Marinate the chicken for a minimum of 2 hours, or overnight, in the fridge and try to turn the bag over halfway through.

★ Pre-heat the oven to 200°C/400°F/Gas 6. Line a large baking sheet with foil and top with a piece of baking parchment. Remove the chicken from the marinade and sit the drumettes on the prepared baking sheet. Season with salt and pepper and bake for 30 minutes, turning halfway through.

★ Pour the marinade from the bag into a small saucepan. Bring to the boil and boil hard for 3–4 minutes, until thick and syrupy, then leave to cool slightly.

★ Brush the cooked chicken with the cooked and syrupy marinade (do not use the marinade without boiling it first) and sprinkle over the sesame seeds, if using. Let the chicken cool slightly before serving.

Party planning
The chicken can be frozen in the marinade up to 1 month in advance. Defrost in the fridge overnight before cooking.

movie star sleepover

1 Party invitations

Cut out cards approx. 14 x 9 cm (5½ x 3½ in) from stiff black paper and cut rounded edges. Cut out strips of black card about 1 cm (½ in) deep. Draw on a clapperboard design and write the party details on the back of the card. Finally, attach the strip to the bottom of the larger card using a gold paper fastener. For place settings, use a VIP backstage pass with each guest's name on.

2 Starry eyes
Budding movie stars can decorate
cheap sunglasses with stars, sequins,
glitter and feathers, and the children
can dress up as their favourite movie
star or character.

3 Guess the star
Each person secretly writes the name
of a famous star or cartoon character
on a sticker. Without showing your
friend the sticker, place it on her
forehead. She has to guess which star
she is by asking questions that can
only be answered with a yes or no!

chicken caesar salad

Caesar salad was invented by Caesar Cardini, who owned a restaurant in Los Angeles in the 1930s. The salad first became famous because it was loved by movie stars of the time, but it continues to be a favourite today. Serve this finger-food variation in wraps or small lettuce cups.

Makes 4 portions

2 slices white or brown bread

2 tbsp sunflower oil

4 tbsp mayonnaise

2 tbsp Greek yoghurt

15 g (½ oz) grated Parmesan, plus extra to serve

1 tsp lemon juice

3–4 drops Worcestershire sauce (or to taste)

salt and pepper, to season

225 g (8 oz) cooked chicken, diced

8 Little Gem leaves

4 flour tortilla wraps (if making wraps)

Party planning

The croûtons can be made a day ahead and stored in an airtight box. The chicken salad can also be made a day in advance and stored, covered, in the fridge until needed.

★ Pre-heat the oven to 180°C/350°F/Gas 4. Cut star shapes from the bread using a small star-shaped cutter (or trim off the crusts and cut the slices into 1 cm/½ in cubes) and put in a bowl. Drizzle over the oil and toss until coated. Spread the bread out on a baking sheet and bake for 5 minutes. Carefully turn the croûtons over and bake for a further 5–8 minutes, until golden, watching carefully. Leave to cool.

★ Mix together the mayonnaise, yoghurt, Parmesan, lemon juice and Worcestershire sauce and season to taste with salt and pepper. Stir in the cooked chicken.

★ To serve in lettuce cups: divide the chicken salad between the Little Gem leaves. Sprinkle each with a little grated Parmesan and a few croûtons.

★ To serve as wraps: warm the wraps in a microwave for 5–10 seconds or place in a warm oven for 5 minutes. Meanwhile, finely shred the lettuce leaves. Scatter the lettuce down the centre of the wraps and spoon the chicken salad over. Sprinkle each with a little grated Parmesan and a few croûtons, roll up and serve immediately. You can omit the croûtons from the wrap version if you prefer. It is also fun to roll up each wrap in foil and scrunch one end to seal. The children can then eat the wraps, peeling the foil away as they eat, without worrying about dripping any dressing on the sofa.

crunchy caramel popcorn

This is the best ever recipe for popcorn – a cinema treat loved by everyone.
If you are using microwave popcorn, try to buy the natural, unflavoured type.
Serve in stripy bags or tubs for the full effect. Yum!

Makes 4–6 portions
sunflower oil, for greasing
100 g (3½ oz) popping corn or 1 packet
    of microwave popcorn (natural)
55 g (2 oz) butter
100 g (3½ oz) soft light brown sugar
2 tbsp golden syrup
a pinch of salt

Party planning
The popcorn can be made 1 day
in advance and stored overnight
in an airtight box. Make sure the
corn is completely cold before
covering; if it is warm it will turn
soggy. Also, hide the box – it is
so irresistible it may not last
the night!

★ Pre-heat the oven to 150°C/300°F/Gas 2. Line a large baking sheet with foil and lightly grease with oil. Pop the corn according to the packet instructions. Transfer to a large bowl and leave to cool slightly.
★ Put the butter, sugar and syrup in a saucepan with 2 tablespoons of water and the salt. Heat gently until the butter has melted and the sugar has dissolved, then bring to the boil and remove the syrup from the heat.
★ Let the syrup cool slightly, then drizzle over the popcorn. Toss the popcorn carefully to coat in the syrup – use 2 large wooden spoons or salad servers to do this. Spread the popcorn out over the prepared baking sheet and bake in the oven for 15 minutes. Remove and carefully stir the popcorn, then bake for a further 15 minutes, watching closely for the last 5 minutes as the sugar can brown very quickly towards the end of the cooking time.
★ Remove the popcorn from the oven and let it cool on the baking sheet for 5 minutes, then transfer to a bowl and serve warm (check the temperature before serving as the caramel coating can stay hot for a while) or leave to cool completely (it will crisp up as it cools).

banana chocolate-chip pancakes

Banana chocolate-chip pancakes are a star turn at breakfast, lunch …
or any time of day!

**Makes 12 pancakes or 4 portions
(easily doubled)**

1 medium-sized ripe banana

1 egg

3 tbsp clear honey, plus extra
    to serve

½ tsp vanilla extract

3 tbsp milk

110 g (4 oz) self-raising flour

½ tsp bicarbonate of soda

a pinch of salt

30 g (1 oz) milk chocolate,
    chopped fine or small chips

sunflower oil, for frying

2 bananas, sliced, to serve

whipped cream or Greek yoghurt,
    to serve (optional)

★ Mash the ripe banana in a bowl until smooth then whisk in the
egg, honey, vanilla and milk. In another, large, bowl, mix together the
flour, bicarbonate of soda and salt and make a well in the middle. Pour
the banana mixture into the well and stir to make a smooth batter. Fold
in the chocolate chips and leave the batter to stand for 5 minutes.

★ Meanwhile, pre-heat the oven to its lowest setting and put a large,
heavy-based, non-stick frying pan over a medium–low heat (when cooking
these, the temperature of the pan needs to be slightly lower than normal
for cooking pancakes, as the banana and chocolate in them can colour
too quickly and burn the outside). Grease lightly with oil then drop 2
tablespoons of batter into the pan. Cook the pancake for 2–3 minutes
or until golden underneath and bubbling on top. Flip the pancake and
cook for a further 2–3 minutes or until cooked through.

★ Cook the pancakes in batches of 2–4 (depending on the size of your
pan), transfer to a plate and keep warm in the oven until all of the batter
has been used up.

★ Serve the pancakes in stacks with sliced bananas and drizzled with a
little extra honey plus a dollop of whipped cream or Greek yoghurt, if liked.

hollywood sunset strip mocktail

Sunset Strip in Hollywood is a road famous for cafés where you will find every self-respecting starlet sipping her sunset-hued mocktail.

Makes 1 drink
200 ml (7 fl oz) chilled tropical
  fruit juice
½ tsp grenadine syrup

★ Pour the fruit juice into a tall glass (a champagne flute is perfect, but a tall water glass will also be fine). Slowly add the grenadine; it will sink to the bottom and mix with the juice to make a sunset-coloured drink, graduating from orange through to red. You can stir slightly before drinking, if you like.

croissants cordon bleu

Ordinary croissants are given movie-star treatment with cheese and ham. For non meat-eating princesses, omit the ham.

Makes 4 croissants – large ones would make 8 portions (easily halved)
40 g (1½ oz) butter
40 g (1½ oz) plain flour
300 ml (½ pint) milk
½ tsp Dijon mustard
1 egg yolk
salt and pepper, to taste
4 croissants
55 g (2 oz) grated Gruyère
55 g (2 oz) grated Cheddar
4 slices ham
2 tbsp grated Parmesan

Party planning
Make the sauce 1 day ahead, transfer to a bowl and press a piece of cling film onto the surface of the sauce. Chill until needed.

★ Melt the butter in a saucepan, stir in the flour and cook the paste for 1 minute. Remove from the heat and whisk in the milk, a little at a time, until you have a smooth sauce.
★ Put the saucepan over a medium heat and bring to the boil, whisking constantly. It will be a very thick sauce, and it needs to be, otherwise it makes the croissants soggy. Cook for 1 minute, still stirring, then remove from the heat and stir in the mustard and egg yolk. Season to taste with salt and pepper and cool slightly.
★ Pre-heat the oven to 180°C/350°F/Gas 4. Cut the croissants in half horizontally and spread the sauce over the cut surfaces. Sit the 4 croissant bases on a baking sheet and scatter over half of the Gruyère and Cheddar cheeses. Lay a slice of ham on each base then top with the remaining Gruyère and Cheddar.
★ Sandwich the ham and cheese with the tops of the croissants and sprinkle over the Parmesan. Bake for 18–20 minutes, until the cheese is gooey and the croissants are crisp. Serve warm.

red carpet hollywood star

**Three-layered cakes
(pink, vanilla and chocolate)**
340 g (12 oz) caster sugar
340 g (12 oz) butter, at room
    temperature, plus extra
    for greasing
6 eggs
1 tbsp vanilla extract
340 g (12 oz) self-raising flour
¼ tsp salt
5 drops of red food colouring,
    plus extra for buttercream
2 tbsp cocoa powder

Candy stars
100 g (3½ oz) red boiled sweets
100 g (3½ oz) yellow boiled sweets
2 tbsp vegetable oil for greasing
edible silver or gold balls

Decoration
½ x 500g carton of chocolate
    buttercream
1 x 500g carton of vanilla buttercream
edible silver or gold balls
writing icing
red, orange and yellow M&Ms
a doll for an actress
60 cm (24 in) red ribbon, about 4cm
    (1½ in) width
alphabet candles

You will also need star-shaped cutters

⭐ To make the sponge cakes, first pre-heat the oven to 180°C/350°F/Gas 4. Grease 3 x 20 cm (8 in) sandwich tins and line the bases with baking parchment. Cream together the sugar and butter until pale and fluffy. In a separate bowl, beat the eggs and vanilla together and add to the butter and sugar a little at a time. Sift together the flour and salt and fold into the butter mixture. Mix thoroughly.

⭐ Divide the cake mixture equally between three bowls. Colour one batch with red food colouring – dip the end of a teaspoon into the food colouring and add 5 drops, one at a time, mixing well. Using a fine sieve, gradually add the cocoa to the second bowl, mixing well. Set aside the third bowl.

⭐ Pour the three cake mixtures into separate sandwich tins and bake for 25–30 minutes until risen and firm to the touch. Allow to cool slightly, then turn out onto a wire rack and leave to cool completely.

⭐ Meanwhile, prepare the candy stars. Pre-heat the oven to 150°C/300°F/Gas 2. Tip the boiled sweets into a double-layered freezer bag and bash with a rolling pin to make fine, small pieces. Dip the star-shaped cutters in oil then place on a baking sheet lined with baking parchment. Spoon the crushed sweets into the oiled cutters to a depth of about 3 mm (⅛ in). Bake for about 8–10 minutes. Remove from the oven and scatter over the silver or gold balls. Leave to cool for about 15 minutes before carefully removing the candies from the cutters (use a tea towel to protect your hands). You can make 8–10 star candies depending on the size of the cutters.

⭐ Beat half of the vanilla buttercream with 3–5 drops of red food colouring. Layer the cakes, sandwiching them together with chocolate buttercream and the next layer with vanilla buttercream, then spread pink buttercream on the top. Leave for 2–3 hours to allow the surface to harden slightly.

⭐ Add silver and gold balls around the sides of the top and bottom cakes, using blobs of writing icing, and arrange red, orange and yellow M&Ms around the middle cake. For the final touch, place red ribbon down the centre of the cake. Just before serving, put the candles at the back and the candy stars at the front. Place your princess's favourite actress on the red carpet for the awards ceremony.

princess soda fountain

chocolate malted milkshake

My deluxe version of this shake includes both chocolate and ice cream – using vanilla ice cream makes this a 'black-and-white' shake (half-chocolate and half-vanilla) and using chocolate ice cream makes it a 'double chocolate' shake. For chocolate milk, just stir half of the base mixture into a 150 ml (5 fl oz) glass of milk (or hot milk for hot chocolate!).

Makes 2 large shakes (easily increased)

Base

55 g (2 oz) plain chocolate, chopped
2 tbsp malted milk powder (Ovaltine)
2 tbsp golden syrup
4 tbsp milk

Shake

200 ml (7 fl oz) milk
2 large scoops ice cream, vanilla
    or chocolate

Party planning

The base can be made up to 2 days ahead. Chill in a jam jar or covered container until needed.

★ Put all the ingredients for the base into a small saucepan. Heat very gently, stirring constantly, until the chocolate has almost melted. Remove from the heat and continue to stir until the chocolate has fully melted and the mixture is smooth. Set aside to cool.

★ Put the milk and ice cream in a blender and add the chocolate base. Whiz for about 1 minute or until frothy. Pour into tall glasses and serve with straws.

hot dogs with sticky balsamic onions

A hot dog needs good accompaniments, and although fried onions are nice, kids really love the flavour of red onions cooked in a sticky balsamic glaze.

Makes 4 portions (easily doubled)
2 tbsp olive oil
2 large red onions, thinly sliced
¼ tsp fresh thyme leaves (optional)
2 tbsp balsamic vinegar
1 tbsp soft light brown sugar
salt and pepper, to season
4 good-quality sausages
4 hot dog buns
ketchup, to serve
mild mustard, to serve

Party planning
The onions can be made 1 day ahead and kept in the fridge until needed. Reheat in a microwave for 30 seconds–1 minute, or in a saucepan over a medium heat for 3–4 minutes, stirring frequently. If making larger quantities it may be easier to cook them in separate batches.

★ Heat the oil in a large frying pan and add the onions (it will look like a lot of onions, but they do cook down). Cook the onions over a medium-high heat, stirring frequently, for 15–20 minutes or until very soft.

★ Add the thyme (if using) and balsamic vinegar and cook for 2–3 minutes or until the vinegar has evaporated. Stir in the sugar until dissolved and season to taste with salt and pepper. Keep warm.

★ Grill the sausages for 4–5 minutes each side, until cooked through. Split the hot dog buns lengthways along the top, but don't cut all the way through. Open the buns out like a book and lightly toast. Divide the onions between the buns and nestle the sausages in on top of the onions. Serve with swirls of ketchup and mustard – and a napkin!

skinny oven chips

Skinny chips are a perfect accompaniment to burgers. Baking instead of frying makes the fries healthier, as well as easier to prepare in large numbers.

Makes 8 portions (easily halved)
4 large baking potatoes (total weight
  about 1.2 kg/2 ½ lbs)
100 ml (3½ fl oz) sunflower oil
salt, to season (optional)

Party planning
Cut up the chips up to 4 hours ahead and submerge in cold water. When you are ready to cook them, rinse them and continue as above.

★ Pre-heat the oven to 200°C/400°F/Gas 6. Line 2 large baking sheets with baking parchment.

★ Peel the potatoes and cut them lengthwise into slices ½ cm (¼ in) thick. Cut these slices lengthwise again into chips ½ cm (¼ in) thick. Put the chips in a colander and rinse well with cold water, then pat them dry with a clean tea towel and transfer to a large bowl.

★ Brush the baking parchment with a little of the oil, then add the rest to the potatoes and toss until the chips are thoroughly coated. Lay the chips on the baking sheets in a single layer and bake for 10 minutes. Turn over and bake for another 10 minutes or until golden brown. Sprinkle with a little salt, if liked, before serving.

my mashed potatoes

Makes 6–8 portions
700 g (1 lb 9 oz) potatoes, peeled
  and cut into 5 cm (2 in) chunks
45 g (1½ oz) butter
100 ml (3½ fl oz) milk
4 tbsp crème fraîche or double cream
salt and white pepper, to season
grated nutmeg (optional)

Party planning
The potatoes can be peeled up to 6 hours ahead and submerged in water until ready to cook.

★ Put the potatoes in a large pan of salted water and bring to the boil. Lower the heat slightly and simmer for around 15 minutes, until the potatoes feel tender when tested with a table knife. Drain well then return to the pan and leave to sit for 5 minutes (so that the steam can escape).

★ Meanwhile, warm the butter, milk and crème fraîche or double cream in a small saucepan. Mash the potatoes then add the milk mixture and season to taste with salt, white pepper and grated nutmeg, if using. Beat well with a wooden spoon until smooth.

1 Diner menus

Print out your own diner menu – add a picture of a cool car or jukebox, and list the drinks and food that you're serving at the party.

2 Party invitations

Buy some old vinyl singles. Cut out circles from black card or paper. Write the details of the party on each card circle using a silver pen and glue it in the middle of the record.

princess soda fountain

3 Diner food
Have fun making your own ice cream sundaes and decorating them individually (see page 83). Cut out the cheese stars for your burgers (see page 76).

4 Dressing up
Dress up fifties-style - with poodle skirts, leather jackets, shades, neckscarves and pony-tails.

star burger

A good burger is hard to beat and this one is a star! Ready-sliced cheese from the supermarket is good for the topping, just make sure they are the regular Cheddar ones, not the processed versions.

Makes 8 (easily halved)

Burgers

1 tbsp sunflower oil, plus extra
    for frying
1 small red onion, finely chopped
    (about 100 g/3½ oz)
1 garlic clove, crushed
450 g (1 lb) lean minced beef
40 g (1½ oz) fresh white breadcrumbs
    (made from about 4 slices of bread,
    crusts removed)
½ tsp Worcestershire sauce
4 tbsp tomato ketchup, plus extra
    to serve
3 tbsp grated Parmesan
2 tsp clear honey
½ tsp fresh thyme leaves, chopped
salt and pepper, to taste

To serve

8 large slices of cheese
    (each 7 cm/2¾ in square)
8 burger buns
mayonnaise
1 beefsteak tomato, thinly sliced
8 large Little Gem leaves
sliced gherkins

You will also need one star-shaped cookie cutter 7 cm (2¾ in) – measured tip to tip

★ Heat the oil in a medium frying pan and sauté the onion for 5–6 minutes, until soft. Add the garlic and cook for 1 minute, then transfer to a bowl and leave to cool.

★ Add the beef, breadcrumbs, Worcestershire sauce, ketchup, Parmesan, honey and thyme to the bowl and season to taste with salt and pepper. Mix together and divide into 8 equal portions.

★ Line a large baking sheet with baking parchment. Form 1 burger from each portion of meat mixture by rolling it into a ball between your hands and gently pressing it down onto the baking sheet to slightly flatten it. Cover and place in the fridge until ready to cook.

★ Cut 8 star shapes from the slices of cheese, using the star-shaped cutter (keep the cheese trimmings to use in sandwiches or sauces).

★ To cook the burgers, heat a thin layer of oil in the bottom of a large non-stick frying pan. Fry the burgers for 5 minutes then carefully flip over using a fish slice and fry for 4–5 minutes or until cooked through. You may need to cook them in batches.

★ Top each burger with a cheese star. Split and lightly toast the buns and serve each burger with mayonnaise, ketchup, slices of tomato, lettuce leaves and gherkins (according to each child's preference).

Party planning

Make the burgers up to 1 month ahead. Freeze them on the baking sheet then transfer to a box when frozen. Defrost by placing them on a baking sheet lined with baking parchment and leave them, covered, overnight in the fridge.

diner blue plate special meatloaf

A 'blue plate' is a diner's daily special menu item and meatloaf is usually a popular choice. I like mine with a barbecue sauce and plenty of creamy mashed potatoes.

Makes 6–8 portions

1 tbsp olive oil, plus extra for greasing
2 red onions, finely chopped
1 garlic clove, crushed
200 ml (7 fl oz) tomato ketchup
2 tbsp soft light brown sugar
2 tbsp runny honey or maple syrup
2 tsp Worcestershire sauce
4 tbsp orange juice
85 g (3 oz) fresh white breadcrumbs
   (made from about 4 slices of bread,
   crusts removed)
3 tbsp milk
½ tsp fresh thyme leaves or ¼ tsp dried
1 small carrot, grated (45 g/1½ oz)
½ apple, peeled, cored and grated
   (75 g/2¾ oz)
450 g (1 lb) lean minced beef
salt and pepper, to season

Party planning

The meatloaf and sauce can be prepared 1 day ahead and kept in the fridge, covered, until ready to cook.

★ Pre-heat the oven to 180°C/350°F/Gas 4. Lightly grease a baking sheet.

★ Heat the oil in a medium saucepan and sauté the onions for 6–8 minutes, until soft. Add the garlic and cook for 1 minute, then transfer half of the onion to a bowl and leave to cool. Add the ketchup, sugar, honey or maple syrup, Worcestershire sauce and orange juice to the saucepan.

★ Add the breadcrumbs and milk to the onion in the bowl and stir, then add the remaining ingredients and 3 tablespoons of the sauce. Season to taste with salt and pepper, mix together then transfer to the baking sheet and form into a fat log about 20 cm (8 in) long and 9 cm (4 in) wide.

★ Bake the meatloaf for 30 minutes then brush with some of the sauce. Bake for a further 10 minutes then brush again and bake for 5 minutes. Remove from the oven and leave to rest for 10 minutes.

★ Meanwhile, heat the remaining sauce until boiling and bubble for 1 minute. Serve the meatloaf in slices with the barbecue sauce.

mac and cheese

Baked mac and cheese is a wonderful diner dish, fantastic with a green salad or served as a side with ham or meatloaf. If making individual macs, increase the topping to 60 g (2½ oz) breadcrumbs and 30 g (1 oz) grated Parmesan.

Makes 6–8 portions as a main, or about 10–12 as a side dish
225 g (8 oz) macaroni
45 g (1½ oz) butter, plus extra
    for greasing
45 g (1½ oz) plain flour
600 ml (1 pint) milk
1 tsp Dijon mustard
85 g (3 oz) grated Gruyère
85 g (3 oz) grated mature Cheddar
55 g (2 oz) grated Parmesan
6 tbsp mascarpone cheese
salt and pepper, to season

Topping
40 g (1½ oz) fresh breadcrumbs
    (made from about 2 slices,
    crusts removed)
20 g (½ oz) grated Parmesan

★ Cook the pasta according to the packet instructions. Drain and rinse well under a cold running tap (rinsing the pasta gets rid of any excess starch, which can thicken up the sauce too much), then leave in a colander to drain while you make the sauce.

★ Lightly butter a large baking dish (about 18 x 27 cm/7 x 11 in) or 8 individual baking dishes. Pre-heat the oven to 200°C/400°F/Gas 6.

★ Melt the butter in a large saucepan and stir in the flour to make a smooth paste. Whisk in the milk, a little at a time, until completely incorporated and without lumps. Cook the sauce over a medium heat, whisking constantly, until the sauce thickens and comes to the boil. Allow the sauce to bubble for 1 minute then remove from the heat and whisk in the mustard. Stir in the cheeses until melted, then stir in the mascarpone.

★ Stir the macaroni into the sauce and season well with salt and pepper. Spoon the mac and cheese into the greased baking dish (or dishes). Mix together the breadcrumbs and cheese for the topping and sprinkle over.

★ Put the baking dish (or dishes) on a baking sheet and bake for 15–20 minutes, then finish off under a pre-heated grill for a few minutes until the sauce is hot and bubbling and the topping is crisp.

Party planning
The mac and cheese can be made 1 day in advance and kept in the fridge, covered, until needed. Bake a large dish in an oven pre-heated to 180°C/350°F/Gas 4 for 50 minutes–1 hour or individual ones at 200°C/400°F/Gas 6 for 30–35 minutes until heated through. Check the dish is hot right through by inserting the tip of a knife into the centre of the mac and cheese. Hold it there for 5 seconds then test the tip carefully on your wrist – the tip of the knife should be hot.

tuna melt

A tuna melt sandwich is a diner classic, and here I suggest serving it in traditional style on toasted wholegrain bread. This recipe makes a decent amount of filling, so if you prefer you could stretch this to three sandwiches, using another two slices of toast and about 85 g (3 oz) of cheese. However, it is also delicious as a topping on toasted muffins for smaller children (in which case this will make 4 portions).

Makes 2 portions (easily increased)

1 x 185 g can tuna, drained (in oil or
    water, according to your preference)
2 tbsp tomato ketchup
1 tbsp soured cream
1 tbsp mayonnaise
a squeeze of lemon juice
2 drops Tabasco
1 large spring onion, finely chopped
    (optional)
salt and pepper, to season
4 slices wholegrain bread, toasted
    and lightly buttered
55 g (2 oz) Cheddar, grated
2 handfuls of crisps, to serve

★ Put the tuna in a bowl and flake slightly with a fork. Add the ketchup, soured cream, mayonnaise, lemon juice, Tabasco and spring onion, if using, and season to taste with salt and pepper. Mix together.

★ Pre-heat the grill to high and sit 2 pieces of toast on a grill pan, buttered-side up. Spread the tuna filling over the toast and scatter on the cheese. Grill for 1–2 minutes, until the cheese has melted. Top with the remaining toast and cut each sandwich in half, or quarters, diagonally.

★ Serve each sandwich with a handful of crisps (you can warm the crisps in a low oven for 5 minutes to give a 'just cooked' effect, if you wish).

Party planning

The tuna filling can be made 1 day in advance and kept in the fridge until needed. Stir before using.

new york cheesecake

New York diners sell lots of different cheesecakes, but a classic vanilla is my favourite. This is delicious served with Very Red Raspberry Sauce (page 85), fresh strawberries, or the blackberry sauce from Sleeping Beauty's Pillows (page 128).

Makes 12 portions
150 g (5½ oz) digestive biscuits
85 g (3 oz) butter, melted
3 eggs, separated, plus 1 yolk
600 g (1 lb 5 oz) cream cheese,
    at room temperature
225 g (8 oz) caster sugar
3 tbsp cornflour
2 tsp vanilla extract

★ Pre-heat the oven to 200°C/400°F/Gas 6. Crush the digestive biscuits to crumbs and mix with the melted butter. Press into the base of a 20 cm (8 in) springform cake tin. Chill while you make the filling.

★ Put the egg whites in a bowl and whisk to soft peaks with an electric hand or freestanding mixer. Set aside.

★ Put the cream cheese in a separate bowl and beat with the mixer until smooth then add the sugar, cornflour, vanilla and egg yolks and beat until combined. Fold in half of the egg whites then fold in the remainder. Pour the filling into the tin and put it on a baking sheet.

★ Bake the cheesecake for 10 minutes then turn the oven down to 110°C/220°F/Gas ½ for 35 minutes. Turn off the oven and leave the cheesecake inside for 2 hours, then remove and chill in the fridge overnight.

★ Unmould the cheesecake, slice and serve.

ice-cream sundae bar

What would a soda fountain be without an ice-cream sundae? There are many flavours – banana split, hot fudge, strawberry – but I think children have most fun if they can make their own from a selection of ice cream, sauces and fillings. Below are some suggestions for ingredients, but don't let this limit you if you have your own favourites!

Makes 8 portions

2 x 500 ml (17 fl oz) tubs vanilla
 ice cream
500 ml (17 fl oz) tub chocolate
 ice cream
500 ml (17 fl oz) tub strawberry
 ice cream
Very Red Raspberry Sauce (see page 85)
Butterscotch Sauce (see page 85)
Chocolate Truffle Sauce (see page 85)
4 bananas – sliced (lengthways for
 banana splits)
225 g (8 oz) mixed berries (e.g.
 strawberries, blueberries,
 raspberries)
2 large chocolate brownies, crumbled
4 chocolate chip cookies, crumbled

For the topping

300 ml (½ pint) double cream, whipped
55 g (2 oz) chopped toasted nuts
chocolate or coloured sprinkles
8 maraschino or glacé cherries

★ Layer your choices of fruit, brownies, cookies, ice cream and sauces in tall glasses in whatever order you wish.
★ Top with whipped cream, nuts and sprinkles and crown each sundae with a cherry.

very red raspberry sauce

225 g (8 oz) raspberries, fresh
   or frozen
6 tbsp raspberry jam
   (preferably seedless)
55 g (2 oz) caster sugar, plus
   extra to taste

★ Put the raspberries, jam and sugar in a saucepan and heat gently until the raspberries release their juices. Bring to a boil and bubble for 1 minute, then remove from the heat and allow to cool. Taste and add more sugar if needed, then sieve to remove the seeds. Chill until needed.

Party planning
Make up to 2 days ahead and store in the fridge.

chocolate truffle sauce

85 g (3 oz) milk chocolate, chopped
30 g (1 oz) dark chocolate, chopped
100 ml (3½ fl oz) double cream
2 tbsp brown sugar
½ tsp vanilla extract

★ Put the chocolate, cream and sugar in a saucepan and heat gently, stirring, until the chocolate has melted. Remove from the heat and stir in the vanilla. Serve warm.

Party planning
Make up to 2 days ahead and store in the fridge (it will become thick like a truffle filling). To reheat, microwave in 10-second bursts until warm or heat very gently in a saucepan.

butterscotch sauce

110 g (4 oz) soft light brown sugar
4 tbsp golden syrup
30 g (1 oz) butter
2 tbsp double cream
½ tsp vanilla extract
a large pinch of salt

★ Put the sugar, syrup, butter and cream in a saucepan and heat gently, stirring, until the sugar has dissolved. Bring to the boil and boil for 1 minute, then remove from the heat and stir in the vanilla and salt. Serve warm.

Party planning
Make up to 2 days ahead and store in the fridge. To reheat, microwave in 10-second bursts until warm or heat very gently in a saucepan.

ice-cream cone cakes

Make these fun cakes instead of cupcakes or a traditional birthday cake.
You need the short, flat-bottomed type of ice-cream cone.

Makes 8
8 ice-cream cones
55 g (2 oz) caster sugar
55 g (2 oz) butter, at room temperature
1 egg
1 tbsp milk
½ tsp vanilla extract
55 g (2 oz) self-raising flour
a large pinch of salt
Icing
100 g (3½ oz) butter, at room
    temperature
175 g (6 oz) icing sugar
food colouring (strong colours such
    as red and orange work best)
coloured sprinkles, to decorate

★ Wrap foil around the base of each ice-cream cone so that it will stand
up straight when inserted into the hole of a muffin tin.
★ Cream the sugar and butter until pale and fluffy. Add the egg, milk,
vanilla, flour and salt and beat until just combined. Divide the batter
between the cones (about 2 tablespoons each, they should be half-full
and no more) and bake for 20–25 minutes, until risen and firm to the
touch. Remove from the oven and cool completely in the tin.
★ To make the icing, beat the butter until pale and fluffy then beat in the
icing sugar a little at a time to make a firm icing. Colour with food colouring,
adding it a drop at a time (you can split the icing in half or more and colour
each bit a different colour). Pipe or spoon swirls of icing onto the cakes
and decorate with sprinkles.

Party planning
Make the cakes up to 1 day in advance and store in an airtight container.
Make the icing up to 1 day before and store, covered, at cool room temperature.
Best eaten the day they are decorated.

princess flower fairies

fruit flowers

Fairies like to flit and fly through beautiful blossoms, and they will particularly love these pretty bunches of sweet and fruity flowers.

Kiwi–Raspberry Flowers
2 large firm kiwi fruits
8 raspberries
You will need a 5 cm (2 in) flower-shaped cookie cutter

Pineapple–Melon Flowers
1 large ripe pineapple, all skin removed
1 cantaloupe melon, halved and seeded
You will need a 7½cm (3 in) flower-shaped cookie cutter, and a melon baller. You will also need a round cookie cutter the same diameter (or 1–2 mm larger, but not smaller) as the melon baller (ours were 2½ cm/1 in diameter) and 12 wooden skewers

Chocolate-dipped Strawberry 'Buds'
100 g (3½ oz) white, plain or milk chocolate (according to your preference), chopped into pieces
8 strawberries, hulled
You will also need 8 wooden skewers

Party planning
The chocolate-coated strawberries can be made up to 2 days ahead and stored in a cool place, though not the fridge, until needed. The fruit for the flowers can be cut the day before and stored on plates, tightly covered, in the fridge until needed. The flowers can be assembled 1 hour in advance.

kiwi–raspberry flowers

★ Peel the kiwi fruits and cut 4 round slices approximately 1½ cm (½ in) thick from the centre section of each kiwi fruit (leftover kiwi fruit can be cubed and used in a fruit salad). Cut each slice into a flower shape using the flower-shaped cookie cutter. Arrange the kiwi flowers on a plate and top each one with a raspberry.

pineapple-melon flowers

★ Cut the pineapple into round slices around 1 cm (generous ¼ in) thick. Use the flower-shaped cookie cutter to cut 1 flower from each slice. It may be easier to press the cutter into the pineapple then cut around the shape with a small sharp knife. Use the round cutter to cut a hole in the centre of each flower.
★ Pat the pineapple flowers with kitchen towel to remove excess juice. Carve 12 balls of melon. Make the flower centre by pushing a melon ball through the hole cut in each pineapple piece. Thread each flower onto a skewer (going through the pineapple and the melon) to secure. Cover the skewer with a green straw.

chocolate-dipped strawberry 'buds'

★ Put the chocolate in a heatproof bowl and melt it over, but not in, a pan of warm water, stirring occasionally. Insert the tip of a skewer into a strawberry and hold the fruit over the bowl of chocolate. Spoon melted chocolate over the strawberry, turning it so it is completely coated. Allow the excess chocolate to drip off, then stand the skewer in a glass in a cool place to allow the chocolate to set. Repeat with the remaining strawberries.
★ If you like, you could pipe swirls or squiggles in contrasting melted chocolate over the cooled and set strawberries.

flower fairies' nectar

Little fairies love to dance and sing, then sip on flower nectar when they need some refreshment. (If you don't have time to make this pink lemonade, simply tint a good-quality bought lemonade by adding a few drops of grenadine syrup.)

Makes 8 glasses (1.5 litres/2½ pints)
225 g (8 oz) sugar
200 ml (7 fl oz) warm water
170 g (6 oz) fresh or frozen raspberries
6 large lemons
900 ml (1½ pints) chilled sparkling
    water
ice cubes, edible flowers and sprigs
    of mint, to serve (optional)

Party planning
The syrup can be made up
to 3 days ahead and stored
in the fridge until needed.

★ Put the sugar and warm water in a medium saucepan. Stir over a low heat, until the sugar has dissolved, then bring up to a boil and add the raspberries. Take off the heat and leave to infuse for 10 minutes.

★ Meanwhile, squeeze the lemons and put the juice in a heatproof jug. Strain the raspberry syrup into the jug, pushing the raspberries against the side of the sieve with a wooden spoon to extract as much juice as possible. Chill the lemon-raspberry syrup for 4 hours, or preferably overnight.

★ To serve, add the chilled water to the syrup and stir to combine. Serve in ice-filled glasses with an edible flower and a sprig of mint, if using.

fairy finger sandwiches

Flower fairies will love to nibble daintily on their favourite finger sandwiches.

Makes approx. 8 x 5cm (2 in) sandwiches

Ham and Cream Cheese
2 tbsp cream cheese, slightly softened
1 tsp tomato ketchup
4 slices of bread, lightly buttered
2 large slices ham (approx. 30 g/
   1 oz per slice)

pb&j
1½ tbsp peanut butter (preferably
   smooth)
4 slices of bread, lightly buttered
1 tbsp raspberry jam, plus extra for
   decoration if cutting into shapes

Chicken and Sweetcorn
30 g (1 oz) cooked chicken, diced
2 tbsp drained tinned sweetcorn
1 tbsp mayonnaise
1 tbsp Greek yoghurt
2–3 drops lemon juice
salt and pepper, to season
4 slices bread

Party planning

The sandwiches can be made up to 4 hours ahead, put on plates and covered tightly with cling film. Store in the fridge until needed.

★ To make the sandwiches fit for fairies, I like to roll the unbuttered slices of bread with a rolling pin so that they are about half their original thickness.

★ To make flower and butterfly shapes, spread the fillings on 2 slices of bread and cut the tops from the other 2 slices of bread.

★ Cut out flower centres or spots on butterflies using a round cookie cutter or the end of a piping nozzle. Arrange the bread shapes over the filled slices, then use the cookie cutter to cut out the complete sandwich.

ham and cream cheese

★ Mix together the cream cheese and ketchup and spread over 2 of the slices of bread. Lay the slices of ham on top of the cream cheese, then sandwich with the remaining slices of bread, trim off the crusts and cut into fingers, squares or triangles – or cut into shapes as outlined above.

pb&j

★ Spread the peanut butter over 2 slices of the bread, then spread a thin layer of jam over the peanut butter. Sandwich with the remaining slices of bread, trim off the crusts and cut into fingers, squares or triangles – or cut into shapes as outlined above.

★ If making flower shapes, cut out the bread first, cutting a round hole in the centre of half the shapes. Spread the flowers without holes with peanut butter, spoon a blob of jam in the centre, and cover with the flower slices with holes in so you can see the jam peeping through.

chicken and sweetcorn

★ Mix together the chicken, sweetcorn, mayonnaise and yoghurt. Add the lemon juice and salt and pepper to taste.

★ Spread over 2 of the slices of bread and sandwich with the remaining bread. Trim off the crusts and cut into fingers, squares or triangles – or cut into shapes as outlined above.

strawberry scones

Light-as-air scones topped with a cloud of strawberry mascarpone jam are sweet treats for fluttering fairies.

Makes 12 portions
(each portion is half a scone)

Scones
110 g (4 oz) plain flour, plus
    extra for dusting
1 tbsp caster sugar
1 tsp baking powder
½ tsp bicarbonate of soda
a large pinch of salt
30 g (1 oz) cold butter, cut into
    small cubes
6 tbsp milk, plus 1 tbsp extra
    for glazing

Filling
110 g (4 oz) mascarpone cheese
2 tbsp strawberry jam
110 g (4 oz) strawberries, hulled
    and sliced or chopped

Party planning
The scones can be made up to 1 month in advance and frozen in a re-sealable bag or plastic box. Defrost for around 1 hour at room temperature.

★ Pre-heat the oven to 200°C/400°F/Gas 6. Lightly dust a baking sheet with flour.

★ Stir the flour, sugar, baking powder, bicarbonate of soda and salt together in a bowl. Rub in the butter then stir in the milk to make a soft dough.

★ Roll out the dough to 2 cm (¾ in) thick and cut out circles with a 5 cm (2 in) diameter round cutter. Gather together the trimmings, re-roll and cut more circles to give 6 scones.

★ Put the scones on the prepared baking sheet and brush the tops with the extra milk. Bake for 13–15 minutes, until risen and golden. Transfer to a wire rack to cool.

★ Mix together the mascarpone and strawberry jam. Cut the scones in half and sit the tops cut-side up. Spread the mascarpone jam over the cut sides of the scones and top with the strawberries.

mini blueberry tarts

These are delicious as well as fun to make. You can prepare the tart cases ahead and freeze them. You could also top the tarts with raspberries or a mix of raspberries and blueberries. Unlikely, but if you do have any left over, store them in the fridge away from Dad …

Makes 12 mini tarts

Pastry
85 g (3 oz) plain flour
45 g (1½ oz) cold butter, cut into
   1 cm (½ in) cubes
15 g (½ oz) icing sugar
1 egg yolk
1 tbsp water

Filling and glaze
55 g (2 oz) mascarpone cheese
55 g (2 oz) half-fat crème fraîche
¼ tsp vanilla extract
1 tbsp icing sugar
100 g (3½ oz) small blueberries
2 tbsp seedless raspberry jam
1 tbsp water

★ Put the flour, butter and icing sugar into a food processor. Whiz for about 30 seconds, until it resembles fine sand. Add the egg yolk and water and pulse until it just forms a dough.

★ Pre-heat the oven to 200°C/400°F/Gas 6. Roll out the dough on a lightly floured surface, to about 2 mm (⅛ in) thick. Cut out 6 circles using a 6 cm (2½ in) fluted round cutter. Ease the pastry circles into the holes of a mini muffin tin. Set aside in the fridge for 30 minutes or, if time is short, pop the tin into the freezer for 10 minutes.

★ Prick the base of the pastry cases and bake in the oven for 8–10 minutes (check after 8 minutes). Cool in the tin for 10 minutes then ease them out using the tip of a table knife. Immediately place them in the fridge.

★ Mix together all the filling ingredients except the blueberries and divide between the cooled pastry cases. Top each tart with 5 blueberries. Melt the raspberry jam with the water in a small pan over a low heat, then brush the glaze over the blueberries.

flower fairies

1 Party invitations
Get some plain cards and paper to write your invitation on. Pop a packet of flower seeds inside the envelope, and sew a paper flower onto the outside.

2 Flower chains
Thread and weave flowers together to make pretty daisy chains or buttercup chains.

3 Place settings

Use mini flower pots for each setting – either paint each guest's name on the pot or on a lolly stick. Add some disposable cutlery which you can tie up with garden string or twine.

4 Little fairies

Younger princesses can have fun decorating fairy wings and wands, and dressing up in fairy costumes.

flowerpot cakes

Makes 4

Chocolate cakes

110 g (4 oz) butter, at room temperature,
 plus extra for greasing

110 g (4 oz) caster sugar

2 eggs

1 tsp vanilla extract

85 g (3 oz) self-raising flour

4 tbsp cocoa powder

a pinch of salt

Decoration

280 g (10 oz) ready-made light brown
 regal icing, or 280 g (10 oz) ready-
 made white royal icing coloured
 brown by mixing together yellow,
 red and black food colouring

3 tbsp apricot jam

100 g (3½ oz) white chocolate

20 g (¾ oz) desiccated coconut

yellow and orange M&Ms

Some drops of green food colouring
 or ½ tsp Japanese green tea powder

8 wooden skewers

icing sugar, for dusting

*You will also need 4 dariole moulds,
a 900 g (2 lb) loaf tin, a star- or flower-
shaped cookie cutter (about 4 cm/2 in),
a tear-shaped cookie cutter and some
baking parchment*

★ Pre-heat the oven to 180°C/350°F/Gas 4. Grease the dariole moulds and line the bases with circles of baking parchment. Grease the loaf tin and line with baking parchment.

★ Cream together the butter and sugar until pale and fluffy. In a separate bowl, beat together the eggs and vanilla then beat into the butter mixture a little at a time. Sift over the flour, cocoa and salt and fold in well. Divide the mixture between the prepared moulds to half-full. The remaining mixture goes into the loaf tin; spread it evenly, about 1 cm (½ in) thick.

★ Place the dariole moulds and the loaf tin in the oven and bake for 15–17 minutes until risen and firm. Allow to cool, then remove from the dariole moulds and the loaf tin to a wire rack until completely cold.

★ Using a rolling pin, roll out the light brown royal icing to make 20 x 30cm (8 x 12 in) rectangle. Using a sharp knife and a ruler, cut the icing to fit around the sides of the dariole cakes, so they look like pots – about 5–6cm (2–2½ in), depending on how high the cakes are – then make four thin strips, about 1.5cm (1 in) for the pot rims. Re-roll the trimmings to make the strips, if necessary.

★ Warm the apricot jam gently in a small pan and brush the sloped sides of the dariole cakes with the jam. Wrap the brown icing around the cakes, and press gently to help the icing stick to the cake. Trim away the excess. Attach the strips of icing to make a rim on each flowerpot, using a little water if necessary.

★ Using a cookie cutter, cut out four flower shapes and leaves from the loaf-tin cake. Break the white chocolate into small pieces and melt over a bowl of simmering water. Dip one side of the flower cakes into the chocolate and cool on a wire rack. Sprinkle the coconut on top and place an M&M in the centre.

★ Add some drops of the green food colouring or the green tea powder to the rest of the melted chocolate. Dip the leaves into the green chocolate and set aside to harden. To serve, attach the flower and the leaves to the pot using wooden skewers (remove skewers before eating).

tiny tomato tarts

Miniature tarts are the perfect size for delicate fairy fingers, and the sweet cherry tomato filling will delight tiny tastebuds. If you roll the pastry quite thin you will probably be able to make up to 16 mini tarts. You could fill these with strips of ham instead of the cherry tomatoes.

Makes 12–16

Cheese Pastry
85 g (3 oz) plain flour
45 g (1½ oz) cold butter,
    cut into 1 cm (½ in) cubes
30 g (1 oz) grated Parmesan
a small pinch of salt
1 egg yolk
1 tsp water
¼ tsp fresh or a pinch of dried
    thyme (optional)

Filling
8 small cherry tomatoes
1 large egg yolk
3 tbsp double cream or milk
2 tbsp grated Parmesan
salt and pepper, to season

★ Put the flour, butter, Parmesan and salt (only a little – Parmesan is salty) into a food processor. Whiz for about 30 seconds, until it resembles fine sand. Add the egg yolk, water and thyme and pulse until it just forms a dough.

★ Pre-heat the oven to 200°C/400°F/Gas 6. Roll out the dough on a lightly floured surface, to about 2 mm (1/16 in) thick. Cut out circles using a 6 cm (2½ in) fluted round cutter. Ease the pastry circles into the holes of a mini muffin tin. Re-roll the trimmings as required. Set the pastry cases aside in the fridge for 30 minutes or, if time is short, pop the tin into the freezer for 10 minutes.

★ Cut the tomatoes in half. Whisk together the egg yolk, cream or milk and 1 tablespoon of the Parmesan and season with pepper and a very small pinch of salt. Put about ½ teaspoon of egg mixture in each pastry case and sit the tomatoes on top – cut-side up. Sprinkle over the remaining Parmesan.

★ Bake the tarts for 15–16 minutes, until the pastry is golden around the edges. Leave to cool for 10 minutes in the tins before easing them out using the tip of a table knife. Serve warm or at room temperature.

Party planning
The pastry can be made up to 1 month in advance and frozen, wrapped tightly in cling film. Defrost overnight in the fridge and use as above. The tarts can be made a day ahead, then put in the fridge once cool. Re-heat in a low oven for 10–15 minutes. You can use 150 g (5½ oz) of ready-made pastry if you prefer, and increase the Parmesan in the filling to 3 tablespoons.

fairy tutus

Crisp meringues are like fairy tutus – light as air and they can disappear in a flutter!

Makes 8 tutus
3 egg whites
a pinch of salt
170 g (6 oz) caster sugar
2–3 drops red food colouring
150 ml (5 fl oz) double cream
110 g (4 oz) blueberries
8 strawberries, hulled and cut
  lengthways into slices

Party planning
The meringues can be made 1–2
days in advance and stored in an
airtight box. They will soften more
quickly in humid weather.

★ Measure out 2 pieces of baking parchment to fit 2 baking sheets.
Draw 4 circles of 6–7 cm (2½–3 in) diameter (a round cutter is good as
a guide) on each piece of parchment 5 cm (2 in) apart. Turn the parchment
over and put one piece on each baking sheet, so the circles show through
but the ink side is face down.

★ Pre-heat the oven to 110°C/225°F/Gas ¼. Put the egg whites in a clean
bowl with a pinch of salt and whisk to stiff peaks. Whisk in 2 tablespoons
of the sugar and whisk back to stiff peaks, then whisk in another 1
tablespoon of sugar with the food colouring and whisk back to stiff
peaks. Fold in the remaining sugar.

★ Divide the meringue mixture between the circles on the baking
parchment and use a table knife to spread it out into rounds, using the
circles as a guide. As you spread it out, use the tip of the knife to shape
the edges of the meringue into waves (using a slight rocking motion),
so it looks like a tutu. Make a slight hollow in the centre of each meringue.
(You could also transfer the meringue mixture to a piping bag with a
large star nozzle and pipe a base and the edges of a meringue basket.)

★ Bake the meringue for 1½–2 hours, until the meringue releases from
the baking parchment, then turn the oven off and leave them inside
until completely cold – preferably overnight.

★ Whip the cream to soft peaks and spoon a little into each meringue.
Top with the blueberries and sliced strawberries.

princess
beach babe

huli huli chicken

Huli huli means 'to turn' in Hawaiian, and this may well be the original word for the Hula dance. These yummy chicken skewers are turned on the barbecue until golden and sticky. The chicken can be cut into cubes, if preferred.

Makes 8 skewers
8 chicken mini fillets (or approx. 340 g/12 oz of chicken breast fillet, cut into 8 long strips)

Marinade
100 ml (3½ fl oz) pineapple juice
2 tbsp soy sauce
1 tsp grated fresh root ginger
2 tbsp runny honey

You will also need 8 wooden skewers, soaked in water for at least 30 minutes

★ Whisk the marinade ingredients together in a medium bowl. Add the chicken and stir to make sure the chicken is coated in the marinade, then cover and leave to marinate in the fridge for 1 hour.

★ Remove the chicken from the marinade and thread onto the skewers. Pour the marinade into a saucepan and boil over a high heat to reduce, until thickened to a coating consistency. Barbecue the chicken over medium–hot coals for 6–7 minutes, until the chicken is just cooked. Brush the chicken generously all over with the reduced marinade and barbecue for 1 minute, then brush with the marinade again and barbecue for 1 more minute. Cool slightly before serving.

★ Alternatively, if you are not barbecuing, pre-heat the grill and cook the skewers under the grill for 3–4 minutes each side. Reduce the marinade until thickened (as above), then brush the chicken for the last minute under the grill.

hawaiian skewers

Warm and juicy pineapple pieces wrapped in crisp bacon make these
'Hawaiians on Horseback' delicious snacks for a beach party. Leftover
pineapple can be used in fruit salad.

Makes 8 skewers
¼ ripe fresh pineapple,
**   skin and core removed**
8 rashers of thin-cut streaky
**   bacon (pancetta is good)**

You will also need 8 wooden
skewers, soaked in water for
at least 30 minutes

Party planning
The bacon can be wrapped around
the pineapple cubes up to 1 day
 in advance and left in the fridge,
covered, until needed.

★ Cut 16 x 1½cm (½ in) square cubes from the pineapple. Cut the rashers
of bacon in half. Wrap each pineapple cube in a piece of bacon, making
sure the bacon overlaps slightly (it will shrink on cooking).
★ Thread 2 bacon-wrapped pineapple cubes onto each skewer, making
sure the skewer secures the bacon.
★ Barbecue the skewers for 4–5 minutes, turning the skewers regularly,
until the bacon is cooked through and turning crisp at the edges. (The
skewers can also be cooked under a hot grill, see opposite.) Cool slightly
before serving.

coconut prawn skewers

Succulent seafood is a mainstay of the South Pacific islands and perfect for a barbecue, as it cooks quickly. I have added some red onions to make the skewers look a bit more interesting, but you can leave them out if you prefer. If you butterfly the prawns (make a deep cut down the back) they curve nicely. Leave the tails on for a more attractive presentation.

Makes 8 skewers
100 ml (3½ fl oz) creamed coconut
juice of ½ lime
2 tsp soy sauce
2 tsp sweet chilli sauce, or honey
1 tsp grated fresh ginger
1 garlic clove, crushed
freshly ground black pepper, to season
16 extra-large raw prawns (approx. 300 g/10½ oz), shells removed and de-veined
1 red onion, cut into thin wedges (optional)
lime wedges, to serve

You will also need 8 wooden skewers, soaked in water for at least 30 minutes

★ Mix together the creamed coconut, lime juice, soy and sweet chilli sauces (or honey), ginger and garlic with a little black pepper. Add the prawns and toss to coat, then cover and marinate in the fridge for a minimum of 2 hours, or preferably overnight.

★ Remove the prawns from the marinade. Thread 1 piece of red onion onto a skewer (if using), followed by a prawn, another piece of red onion, a second prawn and finally a third piece of red onion.

★ Barbecue the skewers over medium–hot coals for 3 minutes, then turn and cook for another 2–3 minutes, until the prawns are pink and cooked through and the spring onions are soft. The skewers can also be cooked under a grill that has been pre-heated to high.

★ Serve with lime wedges.

polynesian pork ribs (char sui ribs)

The South Pacific islanders love to barbecue; their favourite flavours were influenced by Chinese traders who sailed across the seas. Beach babes will adore nibbling on these sticky, spicy, char sui-style ribs.

Makes 8 portions as part of a luau platter, or 3–4 portions as a main meal

Marinade
45 g (1½ oz) soft dark brown sugar
2 tbsp tomato ketchup
4 tbsp clear honey
½ tsp Chinese five spice powder
2 tbsp mirin
1 garlic clove, crushed
2 tsp grated fresh root ginger
½ tbsp soy sauce

1 kg (2¼ lbs) spare ribs
   (cut into individual ribs)

Party planning
The bag of ribs and marinade can be frozen up to 1 month in advance. Defrost for 24 hours in the fridge and cook as above.

★ Mix together all of the marinade ingredients until the sugar has dissolved. Put the ribs in a large re-sealable bag or a bowl and pour over the marinade. Remove any excess air from the bag, if using, and seal tightly. Make sure the ribs are all coated in the marinade, then place the bag in a bowl and marinate in the fridge overnight. If you are just marinating in a bowl, toss the ribs 2–3 times during marinating.

★ Pre-heat the oven to 180°C/350°F/Gas 4. Line a roasting tin with a double layer of foil (for easier clean up). Remove the ribs from the marinade and sit them in the roasting tin. Pour the marinade into a saucepan and set aside. Cover the roasting tin with foil and bake for 30 minutes. Uncover the ribs, turn them over, re-cover and bake for a further 30 minutes, until the meat is tender.

★ Meanwhile, bring the reserved marinade to a boil and boil hard for 2–3 minutes, until reduced to a syrupy glaze, then set aside. Do not use the marinade as a glaze without boiling it first.

★ Remove the ribs from the roasting tin and barbecue over medium-hot coals for 10–15 minutes, until golden and slightly charred (or grill under a grill pre-heated to high). Transfer to a plate and brush generously with the hot sticky glaze before serving.

ember-baked sweet potatoes

Sweet potatoes are delicious baked and are fun to serve from the glowing embers of a barbecue fire. Spiced up with Parmesan butter and sweet-chilli cream cheese, they are definitely 'hot' potatoes.

Makes 8 portions
8 medium sweet potatoes,
   well scrubbed
Parmesan butter
110 g (4 oz) butter, softened
40 g (1½ oz) grated Parmesan
freshly ground black pepper,
   to season
Sweet-chilli cream cheese
110 g (4 oz) cream cheese
2–3 tsp sweet chilli sauce

Party planning
The Parmesan butter and sweet-chilli cream cheese can be made up to 1 week ahead and stored in the fridge until needed.

★ To make the Parmesan butter, beat the ingredients together with a little freshly ground black pepper until well combined. Form the mixture into a log shape on a piece of cling film, wrap in the cling film and roll into a cylinder shape. Mash together the cream cheese and sweet chilli sauce. Chill both overnight.

★ Wrap each potato separately in a piece of foil. The potatoes need approximately 50–55 minutes baking time, so I prefer to start them off by baking them in an oven pre-heated to 180°C/350°F/Gas 4 for 40 minutes before placing them in the white embers of the fire for 10–15 minutes, turning regularly. If you have a large barbecue, you can bake them entirely in the embers of the fire, turning regularly, then start checking if the potatoes are done after 45 minutes.

★ Unwrap the potatoes carefully and serve with a pat of the butter and a spoonful of the sweet-chilli cream cheese melting in.

princess beach babe

1 Party invitations
Write the details of the party on a piece of paper, roll it up and push it into the neck of a miniature plastic bottle that is filled with a little sand and small shells.

2 Garlands
Make flower garlands from silk or paper flowers threaded onto long pieces of elastic.

3 Beach games
Get the children limbo dancing under a pole and dancing with colourful hula hoops.

4 Grass skirts
You can buy cheap paper grass skirts for the children to wear or make them by cutting up bin bags.

sunset coleslaw

For a party salad, it is difficult to beat a bowlful of colourful coleslaw.

Makes 8 generous portions

¼ small red cabbage, core removed
   and shredded (approx. 110 g/4 oz)
¼ small white cabbage or Chinese
   leaf, shredded (approx. 110 g/4 oz)
2 medium carrots, peeled and grated
   (approx. 110 g/4 oz)
½ red pepper, deseeded and cut
   into matchsticks
85 g (3 oz) sultanas
6 small spring onions, thinly sliced
150 g (5½ oz) mayonnaise
   (reduced fat is fine)
juice of ½ lime
2 tbsp pineapple juice
salt and pepper, to season
1 small eating apple, quartered,
   cored and thinly sliced (optional)

★ Put the cabbages, carrots, red pepper, sultanas and spring
onions in a large bowl.

★ Whisk together the mayonnaise, lime and pineapple juices and
season well with salt and pepper. Spoon over the salad in the bowl
and toss together.

★ Cover and chill for 1–2 hours, then toss again before serving.
If using the apple, add it just before serving as it tends to brown
if left to stand for too long.

tropical smoothie

Delicious fruits grow on tropical islands – mangoes, pineapples and coconuts. Whizzed together they make a luscious smoothie, perfect for sipping on the beach. You could add a squeeze of lime juice, but I like the creamy sweetness of this recipe.

Makes 2 portions (easily increased)
1 small banana, peeled and sliced
   into 2 cm/¾ in chunks
1 large very ripe mango, peeled, pitted
   and cut into 2 cm/¾ in chunks
200 ml (7 fl oz) pineapple juice
2 tbsp vanilla yoghurt
2 tbsp coconut milk
1–2 tsp honey, to taste
slices of fresh pineapple, maraschino
   cherries and umbrellas, to decorate

★ Put the banana and mango chunks in a re-sealable bag and freeze for 3–4 hours, until firm. (This makes a thicker drink, but you can use the fruit unfrozen, if you prefer.)
★ Put the fruit chunks, pineapple juice, yoghurt, coconut milk and 1 teaspoon of honey in a blender and whiz until smooth. Taste, then add the extra teaspoon of honey, if needed.
★ Pour into chilled glasses and decorate with slices of pineapple, maraschino cherries and umbrellas to serve.

Party planning
The fruit can be prepared and frozen up to 1 week in advance.

island beach babe trifle

Jelly
15 sheets of gelatine
400 ml (14 fl oz) elderflower cordial
600 ml (1 pint) water
1 tsp blue food colouring

Fruit
600 g (1 lb 5 oz) various tropical fruits
  (cubed pineapples, dragon fruits,
  bananas, chopped mangoes, etc.)
100 ml (3½ fl oz) orange juice
450 g pot shop-bought custard
250 g (9 oz) mascarpone
zest and juice of 1 lime
4 tbsp sugar

Island
2 large shop-bought Madeira cakes
4 tbsp apricot jam
150 g (5½ oz) green ready-to-roll royal
  icing or 150 g (5½ oz) white ready-
  to-roll royal icing with green food
  colouring to tint

Decoration
3 tbsp demerara sugar
1 small plastic bikini doll
2 or 3 palm tree skewers
1 cocktail umbrella
3 flamingo skewers
seashells
edible pearls
edible flower decorations

*You will also need a round
bowl of diameter 25 cm (10 in),
or a clear tray or baking dish*

★ First, prepare the jelly. Soak the gelatine sheets in a bowl and leave for about 5 minutes. Squeeze out the excess water and place them in a small saucepan. Add the cordial and heat gently until the gelatine is completely melted, stirring well.

★ Pour the water into a bowl and, using a whisk, combine the gelatine mix with the water. Add the food colouring and stir well. For a stronger colour, add a little more colouring. Pour the jelly mixture into the bowl, tray or baking dish. Leave in the fridge for at least 6 hours or overnight.

★ Cut a 1.5 cm (¾ in) thick slice from one of the cakes and set aside. To make the island, put two cakes together and trim off the top of the cakes to make a flat surface, then curve the corners into a rounded island shape using a small serrated knife.

★ Roll out the green icing to about 3 mm (⅛ in) thick and cut to fit on the island to make green grass. Place the green icing on top of the island. (You can smooth out any seams where the icing joins together by dipping a finger in cold water and rubbing gently over the join.) Cut the remaining slice of cake to make a beach for the island.

★ Prepare the fruits and add the orange juice. In another bowl, mix together well the mascarpone, the lime zest and juice, and the sugar. Keep in the fridge until needed.

★ Once the jelly is set, place the island on the jelly, together with the beach. Dampen the edge of the beach with water and sprinkle over the demerara sugar to make it look sandy. Decorate the cake with the doll, the palm trees, flamingoes, etc. Serve alongside the tropical fruits, the custard and the lime mascarpone mixture and let the beach babes make their own trifles.

the princess
and the pea

(and other vegetarian fairytales...)

cinderella's fruit punch

Cinderella went to the ball and sipped on pretty pink drinks with her Prince Charming.

Per drink
75 ml (2½ fl oz) orange juice
75 ml (2½ fl oz) pineapple juice
¼ tsp lemon juice
1 tsp grenadine
a couple of ice cubes
75 ml (2½ fl oz) ginger ale
    or sparkling water
1 maraschino cherry, to decorate

★ Mix the juices and grenadine together in a tall glass (or a glass slipper!) with a couple of ice cubes. Pour in the ginger ale or sparkling water and serve decorated with a maraschino cherry.

cheese stars

Twinkle, twinkle little star, how delicious and cheesy you are!

Makes about 40
110 g (4 oz) plain flour
85 g (3 oz) cold butter, cut into
    small cubes
85 g (3 oz) grated mature Cheddar
30 g (1 oz) grated Parmesan
a large pinch of paprika
salt and pepper, to season
1 egg yolk, beaten with 1 tbsp
    cold water

Party planning
The stars can be made up to 1 month in advance and baked from frozen.

★ Put the flour, butter and cheeses into a food processor with the paprika, a pinch of salt and a grinding of black pepper. Whiz for around 2 minutes, until the mixture forms a dough. Add a couple of drops of the egg mixture, if necessary, to help the dough bind (you should not need more than 1 teaspoon in total).
★ Turn the dough out onto a large piece of cling film and pat into a disc. Wrap in the cling film and chill for around 1 hour, until firm enough to roll.
★ Pre-heat the oven to 180°C/350°F/Gas 4. Roll the dough out on a well-floured work surface to 3 mm (⅛ in) thick and cut stars with a small (about 3½ cm/1¼ in) star cookie cutter. Bring the trimmings together, re-roll and cut more stars until the dough has been used up.
★ Transfer the stars to baking sheets, spacing them about 1 cm (½ in) apart. Brush the stars with the remaining egg mixture and bake for 9–10 minutes, until golden. Cool on the baking sheets for 5 minutes before serving warm, or transfer to a wire rack to cool completely. The baked stars will keep in an airtight box for up to 2 days.

jack's magic vegetables

In Jack and the Beanstalk humble beans are transformed into a magical beanstalk; here, simple vegetables are magically made yummy. Serve with the dips on page 130, or simply with tomato ketchup.

Makes 8 portions

55 g (2 oz) broccoli, broken into small florets

½ courgette, cut lengthways into 8 sticks

½ red pepper, cut lengthways into 8 sticks

1 small onion, cut crosswise into rings

450 ml (15 fl oz) vegetable oil, for frying

55 g (2 oz) plain flour

salt and pepper, to season

2 eggs

100 g (3½ oz) dried breadcrumbs

45 g (½ oz) grated Parmesan

¼ tsp paprika

Party planning

The vegetables can be cut into sticks 1 day in advance. Sit on a plate, cover with a piece of damp kitchen paper and cover with cling film. Chill until needed.

★ Rinse the vegetables with cold water and pat dry thoroughly with kitchen paper. Separate out the onion rings and discard the smaller centre rings (chop and use in another recipe). Put the oil in a deep-fat fryer or in a deep saucepan and heat to 170°C/325°F. Line a large baking sheet with a double layer of kitchen paper.

★ Season the flour with salt and pepper in a shallow bowl. Beat the eggs with a pinch of salt in a separate bowl. Mix the breadcrumbs, Parmesan and paprika together in a third bowl, season with a little salt and some pepper and spread out on a plate.

★ Toss the vegetables in the flour then dip in the egg and roll in the cheesy breadcrumbs until coated. Fry the coated vegetables in the oil for 4–5 minutes, turning regularly, until golden. Cook the vegetables in batches of 4–5 to avoid overcrowding the pan. Remove with a slotted spoon, drain, and transfer to the lined baking sheet while you continue cooking the remaining vegetables.

★ Cool the vegetables slightly and check the temperature before serving, as they can be very hot.

the princess and the pea

1 Mocktails

To decorate the rims of your cocktail glasses, pour coloured sugar onto a small plate. Squeeze or pour some runny honey onto another plate. Dip the rim of the glass into the honey and then into the coloured sugar.

2 Magic broomsticks

Make broomsticks by tying twiglets onto grissini sticks with chives (see page 130).

3 Fruit wands

Thread fruit onto skewers to make magic wands (see page 129).

Once upon a time there was a princess called Mia .... Mia is having a party on Sunday ... Please come & live happily Ever After ....

dress: Fairytail

4 Party invitations

Use a flowing script font and write the invitation like a fairy tale: 'Once Upon A Time, Alice invited all her friends including ... to a party.' Take a damp tea bag and dab it over the paper to stain it. Then enlist an adult's help and burn the edges of the paper to make it look old. It's fun to stamp a seal onto the back of the envelope too, using a little candle wax (again, with an adult's help!).

cinderella's coach risotto

Pumpkins can become wonderful things, like a beautiful coach for Cinderella or a delicious risotto for a princess's supper. For fun, serve this in hollowed-out mini pumpkins or squashes.

Makes 4–6 portions (easily halved)

½ medium butternut squash
  or pumpkin
30 g (1 oz) butter
1 small onion, finely chopped
1 garlic clove, crushed
225 g (8 oz) risotto rice (e.g. arborio)
approx. 900 ml (1½ pints) hot
  vegetable stock
2 tbsp mascarpone cheese
30 g (1 oz) grated Parmesan,
  plus extra to serve
1 tsp lemon juice
salt and pepper, to season
1 tbsp chopped fresh parsley
  (optional), to serve

Party planning

The purée can be made up to 1 month in advance and frozen in a re-sealable container. Defrost overnight in the fridge and reheat gently in a saucepan before using.

★ Peel and deseed the squash and cut into 3 cm (1¼ in) chunks. Steam for 10–15 minutes, until tender. Cool slightly and purée until smooth. Set aside.

★ Melt the butter in a large saucepan and sauté the onion for 5–6 minutes, until soft. Add the garlic and rice and cook, stirring, for a further 2–3 minutes, until the rice is translucent around the edges.

★ Add 300 ml (10 fl oz) of the hot stock and bring to a simmer, stirring frequently, for 8–10 minutes, or until the stock has been absorbed. Add a further 300 ml (10 fl oz) of the hot stock and cook, stirring frequently, for another 8–10 minutes, until the rice is almost tender (if you bite into a grain it will still be slightly chalky in the centre) and the stock has been absorbed. If the rice is still very undercooked, add 100 ml (3 fl oz) more of the stock and continue to cook, as above, for a further 3–4 minutes.

★ Add the squash purée and 100 ml (3 fl oz) of hot stock and cook for 2–3 minutes, until thick. Stir in enough of the remaining stock to give a loose, but not runny, consistency then remove from the heat and stir in the mascarpone, Parmesan and lemon juice. Season to taste with salt and pepper and serve in bowls (or hollowed-out mini pumpkins and squashes) with extra grated Parmesan and sprinkled with chopped parsley, if using.

sleeping beauty's pillows

These plump pancake pillows are filled with sweet cream cheese and served with a sauce made from thorny bush blackberries.

Makes 4 generous portions

Pancakes (or use 8 ready-made pancakes)
110 g (4 oz) plain flour
2 eggs
300 ml (½ pint) milk
a pinch of salt
85 g (3 oz) butter

Filling
200 g (7 oz) cream cheese (reduced fat is fine)
2 tbsp icing sugar
½ tsp vanilla extract

Sauce
340 g (12 oz) blackberries (fresh or frozen)
110 g (4 oz) caster sugar
2 tsp cornflour mixed with 2 tsp cold water

Party planning

The pillows can be made 1 day in advance. Cover with cling film and refrigerate until needed. Brush with a little extra melted butter and bake as above, increasing the baking time to 18–20 minutes. The sauce can be made 1 day in advance and kept in the fridge, covered, until needed. Reheat gently in a saucepan before serving.

★ If making the pancakes, put the flour, eggs and milk in a blender with a pinch of salt. Whiz to make a smooth batter. Pour into a jug and leave to stand for 30 minutes. Meanwhile, melt the butter in a 20 cm (8 in) heavy-based frying pan then pour the butter into a bowl. Set aside 2 tablespoons of the butter and stir another 2 tablespoons into the jug of batter.

★ Heat the frying pan greased with a little of the remaining butter. Pour about 4 tablespoons of the batter into the pan, tilting to coat the base. Make sure there are no holes, otherwise the filling will leak out later. Cook for 1–2 minutes, until golden, then flip the pancake over and cook for a further 1–2 minutes, until there are brown spots on its underside. Grease the pan and cook more pancakes until all of the batter has been used up.

★ The cooked pancakes can be stacked on top of each other on the plate, with a small piece of baking parchment or greaseproof paper between each one. Make 8–9 pancakes, as you will need 8 pancakes for this recipe.

★ Line a baking sheet with baking parchment. Beat together the cream cheese, icing sugar and vanilla. Lay a pancake on a flat surface and put a rounded tablespoonful of the cream cheese mixture in the centre (it is quite rich), spreading it slightly. Fold 2 opposite sides of the pancake into the centre to make a rectangle, then fold the remaining 2 ends in to make a square and enclose the filling. Sit the pancake parcel, fold-side down, on the baking sheet and continue with the 7 remaining pancakes and the rest of the filling. Brush each 'pillow' with a little of the reserved melted butter.

★ To make the sauce, put the blackberries in a pan with the sugar and heat gently until the juice runs and the sugar has dissolved. Crush the blackberries slightly then stir in the cornflour mixture and bring to the boil, stirring, to thicken. Reduce the heat and simmer for 1 minute. The sauce can be used like this or put through a sieve to remove the seeds.

★ To serve, pre-heat the oven to 200°C/400°F/Gas 6 and bake the pillows for 15 minutes. Serve 2 per person with the warm sauce. The filling can be hot, so check the temperature before serving to smaller children.

magic wands

Every good fairy needs a wand – and these will disappear like magic!

Makes 4 (easily doubled)
1 thick slice cantaloupe melon,
  seeds removed
½ ripe mango, sliced lengthways
  into 2 slices about 1 cm (½ in) thick,
  or use 1 star fruit sliced to the same
  thickness as the mango
20 seedless red grapes
  (about 110 g/4 oz)
2 tbsp dulche de leche
2 tbsp Greek yoghurt

*You will also need a melon baller,
a small (about 3½ cm/1¼ in) star-
shaped cutter and 4 wooden skewers*

★ Scoop 4 balls of melon from the cantaloupe using the melonballer and, if you are using mango stars for the wands, cut 4 stars from the mango slices (trimmings from the fruit can be chopped up and added to a fruit salad). If your mango is slightly fibrous you may find it easier to press the star cutter into the mango flesh and trim around the cutter with a sharp knife.

★ Thread 5 grapes lengthways onto each wooden skewer, then add a ball of cantaloupe. Top the fruit wand with a mango star or a star fruit slice, if you prefer. Repeat with the remaining skewers and fruit and chill until needed.

★ Mix together the dulche de leche and yoghurt until smooth. Serve the wands with the dip.

Party planning
The dip can be made 1 day ahead and refrigerated, covered, until needed. The fruit can be cut 1 day ahead (except star fruit, which goes brown) and stored, covered, in the fridge, until needed. Assemble the wands 1–2 hours ahead.

ali baba's gold

This gold is delicious crushed into small pieces and sprinkled over ice cream.

Makes 8 portions
sunflower oil, for greasing
100 g (4 oz) caster sugar
4 tbsp golden syrup
2 tbsp water
½ tsp bicarbonate of soda
  (sieved if lumpy)

★ Grease a large baking sheet with oil and set aside on a heatproof surface. Put the sugar, syrup and water in a deep saucepan and heat gently until the sugar has dissolved. Bring to the boil and boil hard for 4–5 minutes, until the mixture is starting to smoke and has turned slightly darker in colour (if you have a sugar thermometer, you want the temperature to reach 150°C/300°F).

★ Remove the pan from the heat and stir in the bicarbonate of soda. Pour the foaming mixture onto the greased baking sheet and leave to set for 1–2 hours, until cold. When cold break the 'gold' into bite-sized pieces with your hands or by tapping it gently with a rolling pin.

snow white and rose red dips

The two sisters, Snow White and Rose Red, lived in a pretty cottage with their mother. Both were very different, but each was very lovely . . .

Each dip makes 8 portions

Snow White

1 x 400 g can cannellini beans,
   drained and rinsed
½–1 garlic clove (according to taste)
grated zest of 1 large lemon, plus
   3 tbsp lemon juice
2 tbsp olive oil
salt and white pepper, to season
crudités and breadsticks, to serve

Rose Red

50 g (2 oz) drained SunBlush
   tomatoes, oil reserved
1 tbsp tomato ketchup
4 basil leaves
110 g (4 oz) cream cheese
   (reduced-fat is fine)
6 tbsp Greek yoghurt
½ tsp lemon juice
salt and pepper, to season
1–2 tsp milk
crudités and breadsticks, to serve

snow white

★ Put all of the ingredients into a food processor and season to taste with salt and white pepper. Whiz until smooth. Transfer to a bowl, cover and chill until needed. Serve with crudités and breadsticks for dipping.

Party planning

Dip can be made 1 day ahead. Store, covered, in the fridge until needed.

rose red

★ Put all of the ingredients except the milk into a food processor and season with salt and pepper. Whiz until smooth. Add ½ tablespoon of the oil from the tomatoes and 1 teaspoon of milk and whiz again, adding the extra teaspoon of milk if the dip is too thick. Transfer to a bowl, cover and chill until needed. Serve with crudités and breadsticks for dipping.

Party planning

Dip can be made 1 day ahead. Store, covered, in the fridge until needed.

fairy broomsticks

grissini or sesame seed sticks
mini Twiglets or pretzels
string
chives, to decorate

★ Attach mini Twiglets or pretzels to the grissini or sesame seed sticks with a little string so that they look like the twigs on the broomstick, then tie chives around them. The chives are easier to tie if you warm them in the microwave for a few seconds first.

the princess and the pea

Serves 10–12
4 Madeira cakes
6 tbsp strawberry or raspberry jam
200 g (7 oz) buttercream icing
To decorate
icing sugar, for dusting
1 kg packet white ready-to-roll
   royal icing
4 tbsp apricot jam
1 x 500 g packet pink ready-to-roll
   royal icing
sugar flowers
sugar decoration sprinkles
green food colouring
1 doll
1 cake board or tray approx
   25 x 35 cm (10 x 14 in)

★ Cut the cakes in half lengthways and vertically. Spread the strawberry or raspberry jam thinly on one of the cut sides and put the buttercream on top, then sandwich them together. Sit the cakes on their sides on the board or tray, side by side. Trim the tops level so that the cakes fit together snugly to form a rectangle approx 18 x 24 cm (7 x 9½ in).

★ Dust the work surface with icing sugar and roll out 500 g (1 lb 2 oz) of the ready-to-roll white icing to 28 x 34 cm (11 x 13½ in). Warm 3 tablespoons of apricot jam in the microwave (or small saucepan) until runny and brush over the cakes. Cover the cakes with the white icing and trim away any excess icing. Fold the four corners of icing to make it look like a sheet.

★ Use 50 g (2 oz) of the remaining white icing to make a pillow. Make a rectangle shape with a slight dent in the centre, and use your fingers to make a draped edge to the pillowcase. Place on the cake.

★ To make a duvet, dust the worksurface with icing sugar and roll out the remaining 450 g (1 lb) of white icing to approx 24 x 28 cm (9½ x 11 in), slightly thicker than the sheet. Also roll out the pink icing to approx 22 x 28 cm (8½ x 11 in). Place the pink icing on top of the white icing, leaving 2 cm (1 in) on one side. Fold the 2 cm (1 in) of white icing on top of the pink duvet.

★ Place the doll on the bed and cover with the pink duvet. Create drapes around the edges of the bed and trim away any excess icing. Using the apricot jam and a small brush, attach the sugar flowers. Spread the sugar sprinkles around the doll and bed.

★ Use the remaining trimmings of icing to make a pair of slippers and place on the cake board or tray. Finally, using some drops of green food colouring with white icing, make a small pea and tuck it under the mattress.

christmas
angels

iced lemonade

Frozen lemonade – as pure as driven snow. The perfect refreshment for little angels.

Makes 8 portions (easily halved)
4 lemons
225 g (8 oz) sugar, plus extra to taste
600 ml (1 pint) cold water
mint sprigs, to decorate (optional)

Party planning
The lemonade ice cubes can be made up to 1 month in advance. Store in re-sealable bags until needed.

★ Scrub 1 lemon thoroughly and pare off the zest in large strips using a swivel potato peeler. Put the zest, sugar and 250 ml (9 fl oz) of the water in a saucepan. Heat gently, stirring occasionally, until the sugar has dissolved. Bring to the boil and boil for 1 minute, then remove from the heat and leave to cool slightly.

★ Meanwhile, squeeze the juice from all 4 lemons and stir it into the sugar syrup, along with the rest of the water. Strain the lemonade into a clean jug. Freeze the lemonade in ice-cube trays. You can do this in batches: just pop out the frozen lemonade cubes, transfer them to a re-sealable bag and store them in the freezer while you make more. In between batches, keep the liquid lemonade chilled in the fridge.

★ When you are ready to serve, take the lemonade cubes from the freezer and leave them at room temperature for 10 minutes to soften slightly. Put the cubes in a food processor or blender and whiz until the mixture resembles a slushy sorbet. Taste and add more sugar if necessary, whiz once more, then spoon into glasses.

★ Serve with spoons and straws and decorate with sprigs of mint, if liked.

angel cup

A cherubic version of eggnog – and divinely delicious!

Makes 1 portion (easily multiplied)
2 scoops of good-quality vanilla
     ice cream
1/8 tsp good-quality vanilla extract
1 tbsp icing sugar
100 ml (3½ fl oz) cold milk
grated chocolate, cocoa or vanilla
     powder, or grated nutmeg, to dust

★ Put the ice cream, vanilla extract, sugar and milk in a blender and whiz until combined. For a thick shake, use only half of the milk.

★ Pour into a chilled tall glass and sprinkle over a little grated chocolate, cocoa or vanilla powder, or nutmeg, according to taste. Serve immediately.

snowflake sandwiches

Little open snowflake sandwiches will drift away before you know it.

Makes 4 portions (easily doubled)
110 g (4 oz) cream cheese, softened
4 slices white bread
chives, spring onions, carrots, currants,
    sultanas, raisins, chopped pecans
    or walnuts, to decorate

You will also need a 7–8 cm
(3 in) snowflake cookie cutter

Party planning
The sandwiches can be made 1–2
hours in advance. Transfer to a plate
and wrap them tightly in cling film,
then chill until needed.

★ Spread the cream cheese thickly onto the 4 slices of bread and
use a 7–8 cm (3 in) snowflake cutter to cut out snowflake shapes
(you should get 2 per slice of bread).
★ Decorate the snowflakes with your choice of either strips of chives,
thinly sliced spring onions, thin rounds of carrots cut into smaller
snowflake shapes, dried fruits or pieces of chopped nut. Remember,
no two snowflakes have the same pattern!

christmas angels

1 Place cards
Make place cards by punching
a hole in a piece of white card
(or use a white luggage tag).
Add a silver bauble tied on with
white or silver ribbon.

2 Party invitations

Make mini-cards to fit small envelopes and write the details of the party on the card. Stick a name tag on the envelope along with some glittery snowflakes, and tie a ribbon around the envelope.

3 Edible tree decorations

Make the biscuits as described on page 147. You and your guests can have fun decorating them together. Tie ribbon through the holes and hang the biscuits on the Christmas tree.

4 Snowflakes

Make lacy snowflake doilies from white paper by folding it over and cutting out holes.

seraphim's sticky salmon

Skewers of sticky salmon are likely to make your seraphim sing sweetly for second helpings.

Makes 8 skewers – 4 main-course portions (easily doubled)

1 tbsp sesame seeds (optional)

450 g (1 lb) thick-cut salmon fillet, skin removed

2 tbsp plum sauce

2 tbsp clear honey

½ tsp grated fresh root ginger

½ tsp soy sauce

You will also need 8 wooden skewers, soaked in warm water for at least 20 minutes

★ If using, toast the sesame seeds in a hot dry frying pan for 2–3 minutes, then spread out on a plate and leave to cool.

★ Pre-heat the grill to high. Cut the salmon into 1½ cm (½ in) cubes and thread onto the wooden skewers. Lay the skewers on a grill pan lined with foil.

★ Mix together the plum sauce, honey, ginger, and soy sauce. Brush the salmon skewers with this glaze and grill for 2 minutes, then brush with the glaze again and grill for a further 2 minutes. Turn the skewers over and brush with the glaze again, grill for 2 minutes, brush with the glaze for a final time and grill for 2–4 minutes until the salmon is cooked through.

★ Transfer the skewers to a plate and sprinkle with the sesame seeds, if using. Serve warm.

cherub's chowder

On a chilly day little cherubs will like to sip a steaming bowl of delicious chicken and sweetcorn chowder.

Makes 4 portions (easily doubled)
30 g (1 oz) butter
1 small onion, finely chopped
1 medium potato, peeled and diced
    (180 g/6 oz peeled weight)
600 ml (1 pint) chicken or
    vegetable stock
1 x 200 g can sweetcorn, drained
100 ml (3½ fl oz) double cream
100 g (3½ oz) shredded cooked chicken
salt and freshly ground black pepper,
    to season
1 tbsp chopped parsley, to serve
    (optional)

Party planning
The soup can be made up to 1 month in advance and frozen in a re-sealable container. Defrost overnight in the fridge and reheat gently until piping hot. The cooled soup will also keep, covered, in the fridge for 2–3 days.

★ Melt the butter in a large saucepan and sauté the onion for 5–6 minutes, until translucent. Add the potato and cook for a further 3–4 minutes, until the onion is soft. Pour the stock into the saucepan and bring to the boil.

★ Reduce the heat and simmer for 12–15 minutes, until the potato is very soft. Add the sweetcorn and simmer for a further 2–3 minutes. Remove from the heat and cool slightly, then transfer half the soup to a blender and whiz until smooth (take care when blending hot liquids). Pour the blended soup back into the saucepan and stir in the cream and chicken. Season to taste with salt and pepper.

★ Reheat the soup gently until piping hot, then ladle into bowls. Sprinkle each bowl of soup with a little chopped parsley, if using.

cheesy cloud puffs

Plain old popcorn can easily be transformed into savoury light bites.

Makes 6–8 snack-sized portions
100 g (3½ oz) popping corn (1 bag unflavoured microwave popcorn)
30 g (1 oz) melted butter
30 g (1 oz) freshly grated Parmesan
30 g (1 oz) finely grated mature Cheddar
a pinch of paprika (optional)

Party planning
Best served warm, though it can be made up to 4 hours ahead, if necessary.

★ Pre-heat the oven to 220°C/400°F/Gas 6.
★ Pop the corn according to the packet instructions. Transfer to a bowl, cool slightly, then drizzle over the butter and sprinkle over the cheeses. Turn the popcorn gently (clean hands are the best for this) to coat it in the cheese as much as possible, then transfer the popcorn to a large baking sheet, spreading it out in one layer and scattering over any cheese left in the bottom of the bowl. Dust over a little paprika, if using.
★ Bake for 8 minutes, so the popcorn is nice and crisp, stirring halfway through. Transfer to a large bowl to serve.

angel hair pasta

Angel hair pasta is delicate and light – if you can't find it, use vermicelli, capellini or fine spaghetti. Leave out the mushrooms if your children don't like them. You could also use thinly sliced cooked chicken, but you would need to heat it in the microwave first, as the sauce cooks too quickly to heat it through properly.

Makes 4 portions
(easily halved or doubled)
4 slices streaky bacon
2 tbsp olive oil
110 g (4 oz) mushrooms, thinly sliced
salt and pepper, to season
15 g (½ oz) butter
1 garlic clove, crushed
100 ml (3½ fl oz) chicken stock
100 ml (3½ fl oz) double cream
225 g (8 oz) angel hair pasta
2 egg yolks
85 g (3 oz) grated Parmesan,
    plus extra to serve

Party planning
The bacon can be cooked a day ahead and stored, covered, in the fridge until needed.

★ Pre-heat the grill to high and grill the bacon until crisp. Transfer it to a plate lined with kitchen paper and set aside. Put a large saucepan of salted water on to boil.

★ Heat the oil in a frying pan and sauté the mushrooms for around 10 minutes until cooked through, then season to taste with salt and pepper and keep warm.

★ Melt the butter in a small pan and cook the garlic gently for 2–3 minutes, then add the stock and cream. Bring to the boil and boil for 3–4 minutes, until reduced by one-third. Remove from the heat to cool slightly.

★ Cook the pasta in the boiling salted water according to the packet instructions (angel hair usually takes only 4–5 minutes to cook). Meanwhile, put the egg yolks in a bowl and whisk in 4 tablespoons of the warm cream mixture, then whisk in the remaining warm cream and the grated Parmesan.

★ Reserve a teacupful of the pasta cooking water, then drain the pasta and return it to the pan over a very low heat. Immediately add the mushrooms and the egg and cream mixture and toss the pasta. The sauce will thicken with the heat of the pasta, but add a tablespoon or so of the reserved pasta cooking water if the sauce is too thick.

★ Season to taste and serve the pasta on warm plates with the crisp bacon crumbled over and some extra Parmesan.

ice-cream snowballs

You can make all coconut-covered or all chocolate-covered snowballs, if you prefer. These are delicious served with Chocolate Truffle Sauce (see page 85).

Makes 8 snowballs, about 4–8 portions
1 x 500 ml tub good-quality vanilla
   ice cream
1 x 100 g bar white chocolate,
   chilled in the fridge
30 g (1 oz) desiccated coconut
   (covers 4 snowballs)

Party planning
The snowballs can be made 2–3 days ahead and kept frozen until ready to serve.

★ Line a baking sheet with baking parchment and place in the freezer to chill for around 30 minutes.

★ Take the ice cream out of the freezer and leave to soften slightly at room temperature (around 5–10 minutes). Dip an ice-cream scoop in hot water and scoop out a round ball of ice cream, then place it on the chilled baking sheet. Make 7 more ice-cream balls, then immediately put the baking sheet back in the freezer and leave it until the ice cream has hardened again – approximately 4–5 hours or, preferably, overnight.

★ Shave some of the chocolate onto a cold plate using a swivel peeler to scrape shavings from the edge of the bar. If the chocolate becomes too soft, chill it for 10–20 minutes, until firm enough to shave. If you are covering 4 snowballs in chocolate you will need to shave about a quarter of the bar.

★ Spread the coconut out on a second plate.

★ Remove 4 of the frozen ice-cream balls from the baking sheet and roll them in the chocolate shavings. Transfer to a re-sealable box and return to the freezer. Roll the remaining 4 ice-cream balls in the coconut and add to the box with the other balls (or another box if that one is not large enough) and return to the freezer. Keep frozen until ready to serve.

angel cut-out cookies

Decorate these cookies with sparkly balls and gold and silver glitter (available from Squire's Kitchen; see page 158) and hang them from lengths of ribbon to make your own band of angels. For my own princess cookie cutters, go to www.annabelkarmel.com.

Makes 15 large cookies

250 g (9 oz) butter, slightly softened

150 g (5½ oz) caster sugar

1 egg yolk

2 tsp vanilla extract

325 g (11 oz) plain flour, plus extra for dusting

½ tsp salt

340 g (12 oz) royal icing sugar

pink and blue food colouring

silver balls, white sprinkles, edible gold and silver glitter, to decorate

thin ribbon, for threading

Party planning

The unbaked cookies can be frozen on baking sheets lined with baking parchment for 2–3 hours, until solid. Transfer to re-sealable boxes and store for up to 1 month. Bake direct from frozen, following the instructions above and adding 1–2 minutes to the baking time. Baked undecorated cookies can also be frozen in re-sealable boxes for up to 1 month.

★ In a large bowl cream the butter and sugar until pale and fluffy. Add the egg yolk and vanilla extract and beat until combined.

★ Stir the flour and salt together with a fork in a separate bowl, then add to the butter mixture. Mix until it forms a soft dough. Form the dough into a flattish disk, wrap in cling film and refrigerate for at least 30 minutes, or until firm enough to roll out.

★ Pre-heat the oven to 180°C/350°F/Gas 4. Divide the dough in half and roll out one half on a lightly floured surface to 5 mm (¼ in) thick. Cut out cookies with an angel-shaped cutter (or snowflakes, stars, shoes, tiaras etc.). If liked, you can cut out patterns on the cookies using mini cutters and/or the tips of icing nozzles. You can also make a hole in the top of each cookie using the end of a straw, so that you can thread a ribbon through once baked. Repeat with the second half of the dough, then re-roll the trimmings and cut out more cookies.

★ Transfer to baking sheets lined with baking parchment, spacing the cookies about 2½ cm (1 in) apart. Bake the cookies for 11–12 minutes until golden brown. Cool on baking sheets for 5 minutes then transfer to wire racks to cool completely.

★ To ice the biscuits: make up the royal icing according to the packet instructions. Colour one quarter pink and one quarter blue using the food colouring. Transfer the remaining white icing to a piping bag fitted with a narrow (no.1 or no.2) nozzle. Some of the cookies can be iced with coloured icing using a small palette knife, others can be left plain. Pipe patterns on the plain cookies and decorate with gold or silver balls, sprinkles and glitter. Allow the iced cookies to set and then pipe patterns on these. Hang the angels with loops of thin ribbon threaded through the holes.

frosted fruits

Watch out, watch out, Jack Frost is about! Fruits touched with a sprinkle of sparkly sugar make wonderful edible decorations. If you are worried about using uncooked egg white, use dried egg-white powder or meringue powder and make up the equivalent of 1 egg white following the packet instructions.

Makes approx. 10 portions
450 g (1 lb) assorted fruits
  (good fruits include strawberries –
  hulls on, grapes – in bunches of
  3–4 grapes, small plums, physalis,
  cherries and dried fruits such as
  apricots, prunes and pear halves)
1 egg white
approx. 100 g (3½ oz) caster sugar

Party planning
The fruits can be made the night before and kept in the fridge, uncovered, once dry. They will keep for 2–3 days in the fridge.

★ Choose fruits that are firm and unblemished for frosting; it is best to use whole fruits, though, as cut edges tend to release juice which dissolves the sugar. Cut fruit also spoils quickly. Wash any fresh fruit and dry thoroughly with kitchen paper.
★ Put the egg white in a small bowl and whisk with a fork until frothy. Put the sugar in a separate bowl. Using a clean pastry brush, paint a thin coat of egg white on one piece of fruit then dip and roll the fruit in the sugar until coated. Shake off any excess and sit the fruit on a tray or plate. If there are any bald patches, dab a little extra egg white on the patch and dip in sugar again. Continue with the remaining fruit, frosting one piece at a time. Leave the fruits in a cool place to dry for 1–2 hours, then arrange on cakes, desserts or platters.

snowflake cupcakes

These are fun to make at Christmas. You can buy snowflake cookie cutters with small diamond-shaped cutters that can be used to cut holes in the snowflakes. The cakes make great presents, then just pop them into a gift box lined with tissue paper and tie it up with a big silver bow and some Christmas baubles.

Makes 9 cupcakes
85 g (3 oz) plain flour
½ tsp baking powder
    tsp salt
85 g (3 oz) butter, at room
    temperature
¼ tsp vanilla extract
50 ml (2 fl oz) milk
2 egg whites
110 g (4 oz) caster sugar
Icing
3 tsp strawberry jam
100 g (3½ oz) vanilla buttercream
    (ready-made or home-made)
250 g (9 oz) white ready-rolled
    royal icing
edible silver balls to
    decorate (optional)

★ Pre-heat the oven to 180°C/350°F/Gas 4. Sift together the flour, baking powder and salt and set aside.

★ Cream together the butter and vanilla until pale and fluffy. Mix in one-third of the flour mixture, then half the milk, followed by one-third more flour, then the remaining milk, and finishing with the remaining flour. Whisk the eggs whites until foamy. Whisk in the sugar in a stream, then continue to whisk until you get glossy soft peaks. Fold one-third of the egg whites into the butter and flour, then fold in the rest. Spoon the mixture into 9 paper cases set in a 12-hole muffin tin and bake for 20–22 minutes until risen and just firm to the touch. Remove from the oven, cool for 10 minutes in the tin then transfer to a wire rack to cool completely.

★ Once the cupcakes are cool, spread ⅓ teaspoon of the jam over the top of each cake and then cover with 1 tablespoon of the buttercream.

★ Cut out circles the same size as the cake from the white royal icing and also cut out snowflake designs using snowflake cutters. Place the circles of white icing on top of the cupcakes and place the cut-out snowflakes on top. You could also add some edible silver balls for decoration.

yule log

A chocolate roulade is traditional at Christmas and this one's light mascarpone filling is heavenly.

Makes 12 portions

Cake
knob of melted butter, for greasing
6 eggs, separated
a large pinch of salt
150 g (5½ oz) caster sugar
1 tsp vanilla extract
55 g (2 oz) cocoa powder
icing sugar, for dusting

Filling
150 g (5½ oz) mascarpone cheese
50 ml (2 fl oz) double cream
2 tbsp icing sugar
½ tsp vanilla extract

Icing
55 g (2 oz) milk chocolate, chopped
55 g (2 oz) dark chocolate, chopped
170 g (6 oz) butter, softened
150 g (5½ oz) icing sugar

Decoration
icing sugar
white chocolate shavings or
    6 white chocolate truffles
writing icing
edible gold balls
thin red ribbon
holly leaves

★ Pre-heat the oven to 180°C/350°F/Gas 4. Line a Swiss-roll tin with baking parchment, allowing 5 cm (2 in) overhang. Fit the parchment into the corners of the tin, making diagonal cuts inwards from each corner or staple the corners of the parchment together. Brush the base with melted butter.

★ Put the egg whites in a clean bowl with the salt, whisk to soft peaks then set aside. Put the yolks, sugar and vanilla in a large bowl and beat until pale, trebled in volume and mousse-like. Sift over the cocoa powder and fold in a large spoonful of the egg whites. Fold in the remaining egg whites and pour the batter into the prepared tin. Spread the mixture out in an even layer then lightly tap the tin on a work surface a couple of times.

★ Bake for 20–22 minutes, until risen and firm to the touch. Meanwhile, lay a clean tea towel on a flat surface and dust generously with icing sugar. Remove the cake from the oven and allow to cool for 5 minutes. Turn out onto the tea towel and carefully peel off the baking parchment. Take one long edge of the towel and fold it over the long edge of the cake, then roll the cake up in the towel from the long edge and leave to cool completely.

★ To make the filling, briefly beat the mascarpone in a bowl to soften. Add the remaining ingredients and beat for 1–2 minutes until thick.

★ To make the icing, put the chocolates in a bowl sitting over, not in, a pan of warm water. Melt the chocolate, stirring occasionally, then remove from the pan and leave to cool slightly. In another bowl, beat the butter until pale then beat in the melted chocolate followed by the icing sugar. If the icing is very soft, chill for 10–15 minutes.

★ Unroll the cooled cake completely and spread with the filling, leaving a 5 mm (¼ in) border on each short side. Roll up again tightly from the long edge (without the tea towel). Don't worry if the cake cracks a bit, the icing will hide it. Transfer the cake to a serving plate. For a traditional presentation, cut a 10 cm (4 in) piece from one end and sit it on the side of the cake, like a branch, or just leave it as one long Swiss roll. Cover with the icing and use a fork to make 'bark' lines and rings on each end. Chill for 1 hour to allow the icing to set.

The log can be made 1 day ahead and kept in the fridge. Remove 30 minutes before serving. Leftovers will keep for 2 days in the fridge and individual slices can be frozen for up to 1 month. Defrost overnight in the fridge.

★ Decorate with a dusting of icing sugar or shaved white chocolate 'snow' (see page 145 for making chocolate shavings). You could add some mini snowmen by melting some white chocolate and fixing two white chocolate truffles together with a dab of melted chocolate. Draw faces using black writing icing, add a gold ball for the nose, and make a scarf with red ribbon. Add some holly leaves and gold balls to the log and dust with icing sugar

ginger cookie christmas trees

Makes 2 trees

225 g (8 oz) plain flour,
    plus extra for dusting
¼ tsp salt
2 tsp ground ginger
½ tsp baking powder
50 g (2 oz) butter
100 g (3½ oz) soft dark brown sugar
100 g (3½ oz) golden syrup
1 egg yolk
1 tbsp milk
approx. 170 g (6 oz) royal icing sugar

You will also need a set of 6 star cutters in various sizes, ranging from 11½ cm (4½ in) to 2½ cm (1 in)

Party planning

The unbaked cookies can be frozen on baking sheets lined with baking parchment for 2–3 hours, until solid. Transfer to resealable boxes and store for up to 1 month. Bake from frozen, adding 1–2 minutes to the baking time.

★ Sift the flour, salt, ginger and baking powder into a large bowl. Put the butter, sugar and syrup into a pan and heat gently, stirring occasionally, until the butter has melted. Remove from the heat and leave to cool slightly.

★ Beat the egg and milk together and stir into the cooled butter and sugar, then pour the contents of the pan into the dry ingredients and stir to form a soft dough. Transfer onto a piece of cling film and wrap tightly, then refrigerate for 30 minutes–1 hour, or until firm.

★ Preheat the oven to 180°C/350°F/Gas 4. Roll out the dough on a lightly floured surface to around 3 mm (⅛ in) thick. Cut out 4 cookies with the largest cutter, then 4 with the next largest, and so on. Transfer the cookies to baking sheets, spacing them about 2½ cm (1 in) apart and grouping the larger cookies and smaller cookies together on separate sheets. Re-roll the trimmings and cut more cookies as needed. Chill the cookies for 10 minutes in the freezer, then bake for 8–10 minutes for the small cookies and 11–12 minutes for the larger ones, until turning darker around the edges. Cool on the baking sheets for 10 minutes then transfer to wire racks.

★ To assemble the trees, make up the royal icing according to the packet instructions. Take 2 of the largest cookies and sandwich them together with a little of the icing, making sure the tips of the stars are slightly askew. Carefully stack the remaining cookies, in descending size, on top of the base, securing in place with icing. Do the same for the second tree. Reserve the smallest stars for the tops of the trees, but leave to dry for 1 hour before adding the top stars. Stick them together with more icing and drizzle over any remaining icing as decoration. Leave to dry for 5–6 hours before serving.

index

angel hair pasta 144
    Hawaiian skewers 107
    bananas
    chocolate-chip pancakes 64
    tropical smoothie 116–17

beef
    diner blue plate special meatloaf 78–9
    star burgers 76–7
    string of pearls 18
biscuits
    angel cut-out 146–7
    bunny 48–9
    Easter 42–3
    ginger Christmas trees 154–5
blackberry sauce 128
blueberries
    fairy tutus 102–3
    mini tarts 95
boxes, Valentine 29
bunnies 44–5, 47–9
burgers
    little lamb 46
    star 76–7
butternut squash risotto 126–7
butterscotch sauce 83, 85

cakes
    Easter simnel 40–1
    flowerpot 98–9
    ice-cream cone 86–7
    little red velvet 34–5
    princess and the pea 132–3
    red carpet Hollywood
        star 66–7
    Yule log 152–4
    see also cupcakes
cards, Valentine 29
cheese
    angel hair pasta 144
    cheesy clouds puffs 143
    cinema-style nachos 54–5
    croissants cordon bleu 65
    ember-baked sweet potatoes 111

emerald pizzas 10–11
    mac and 80
    pizza hearts 27
    Rose Red dip 130–1
    Sleeping Beauty's pillows 128
    snowflake sandwiches 137
    soufflés 38
    star sandwiches 56
    stars 122
    sweet-chilli cream 111
    tuna melt 81
cheesecake, New York 82
chicken
    Caesar salad 60–1
    cherubs chowder 142
    cupid's arrows 24–5
    golden nuggets 12–13
    huli huli 106
    ruby-glazed 15
    string of pearls 18
    sweet and sticky drumettes 57
    and sweetcorn sandwiches 91
chips, skinny oven 73
chocolate
    -dipped strawberry `buds' 90–1
    banana chocolate-chip pancakes 64
    flowerpot cakes 98–9
    fondue 30
    ice-cream snowballs 145
    malted milkshake 70–1
    nest cupcakes 50–1
    rice krispie hearts 26
    shortbread sweethearts 32–3
    truffle sauce 83, 85
    Yule log 152–4
chowder, cherub's 142
Christmas 134–55
coleslaw, sunset 114–15
couscous, jewelled 14
cranberries
    jewel jellies 19
    jewelled couscous 14
    sparkling ruby cocktail 14
croissants cordon bleu 65

croutons, star-shaped 60–1
cucumber-mint sauce 46
cupcakes
    chocolate nest 50–1
    jewelled 20–1
    snowflake 150–1

dips 24
    maple mustard 12
    Snow White and Rose Red 130–1
    tomato 12
dressing up 59, 75, 97, 113
drinks 14, 30, 65, 70–1, 92, 116–17, 122, 124, 136

Easter 36–51
egg head sandwiches 38–9
egg people 43

flower chains 96
fruit
    Cinderella's punch 122
    flowers 90–1
    frosted 148–9
    wands 125

games 59, 113
ginger biscuits 42, 154–5

ham and cream cheese sandwiches 91
hot cross bunnies 44–5
hot dogs with sticky balsamic onions 72–3

ice-cream
    Ali Baba's gold 129
    angel cup 136
    chocolate malted milkshake 70–1
    cone cakes 86–7
    snowballs 145
    sundaes 75, 83–5
invitations 17, 29, 42, 58, 74, 96–7, 112, 125, 139

jewel jellies 19
jewellery 16–17

kiwi-raspberry flowers 90–1

lamb burgers 46
lemons
  flower fairies' nectar 92
  iced lemonade 136
mac and cheese 80
make-up 16–17
makeovers 17
mango
  magic wands 129
  tropical smoothie 116–17
marinades 12, 24, 106, 110
meatballs, string of pearls 18
meatloaf, diner blue plate special
    78–9
melon
  magic wands 129
  melon-pineapple flowers 90–1
menus 74
meringues, fairy tutus 102–3
milkshakes, chocolate malted 70–1
mocktails 124
  Hollywood sunset strip 65
  mini mimosa 47
  sparkling ruby cocktail 14
muffins
  baby bunny bites 47
  pizza hearts 27
mushrooms
  angel hair pasta 144
  cinema-style nachos 54–5

nachos, cinema-style 54–5

onions, sticky balsamic 72–3
orange juice
  Cinderella's fruit punch 122
  mini mimosa 47

pancakes
  banana chocolate-chip 64
  Sleeping Beauty's pillows 128
Parmesan butter 111

pasta
  angel hair 144
  mac and cheese 80
  passion pink 31
  string of pearls 18
peanut butter and jelly
    sandwiches 93
pineapple
  Cinderella's fruit punch 122
  Hawaiian skewers 107
  pineapple-melon flowers 90–1
  tropical smoothie 116–17
pizza
  emerald 10–11
  hearts 27, 28
place names 17, 42–3, 97, 138
popcorn
  cheesy clouds puffs 143
  crunchy caramel 62–3
pork
  Polynesian ribs 110
  string of pearls 18
potatoes
  cherubs chowder 142
  my mashed 73
  skinny oven chips 73
prawns
  cocktail 56
  coconut skewers 108–9
pumpkin risotto 126–7

raspberries
  flower fairies' nectar 92
  jewel jellies 19
  passion potion 30
  raspberry-kiwi flowers 90–1
  very red raspberry sauce 83, 85
rice krispie hearts 26
risotto, Cinderella's coach 126–7

salad, chicken Caesar 60–1
salmon
  passion pink pasta 31
  Seraphim's sticky 140–1

smoked, and cream cheese
    sandwiches 56
salsa 54–5
sandwiches
  egg head 38–9
  fairy finger 91
  snowflake 137
  star 56
scones, strawberry 94
shortbread sweethearts 32–3
simnel cake, Easter 40–1
smoothies, tropical 116–17
snapdragons 28
snowflakes, paper 139
soufflés, cheese 38
strawberries
  chocolate-dipped `buds' 90–1
  fairy tutus 102–3
  passion potion 30
  scones 94
straws, butterfly 43
sweet potatoes, ember-baked 111
sweetcorn and chicken sandwiches 91

tarts
  mini blueberry 95
  tiny tomato 100–1
tomatoes
  dips 12, 130–1
  passion pink pasta 31
  pizzas 10–11, 27
  string of pearls 18
  tiny tarts 100–1
trifle, island beach babe
    118–19
tuna melt 81
Twiglet broomsticks 125,
    130–1

vegetables, Jack's magic 123
vegetarians 120–33

Yule log 152–4

Annabel Karmel is the UK's best-selling author on baby and children's food and nutrition. She is an expert in devising tasty and nutritious meals for children without the need for parents to spend hours in the kitchen.

A mother of three, Annabel has become a cookbook phenomenon. She has written 18 books on feeding babies, children and families including *Complete Family Meal Planner*, *The Fussy Eaters Recipe Book* and the *After School Meal Planner* and has sold over 4 million copies worldwide. Her *Complete Baby and Toddler Meal Planner* has become the authoritative guide on feeding babies and children and is regularly in the top five cookery bestsellers.

Books are not the only string to Annabel's bow; she now has a range, Make it Easy – food preparation equipment for feeding babies and toddlers, Eat Fussy and World Foods – healthy and nutritious chilled ready meal ranges available in supermarkets, for 1 to 4 year olds and four years + respectively, as well as organic pasta shapes for babies. Along with this, she has developed her own collection of cooking equipment for aspiring junior cooks including Princess Cooking Kits.

Most recently, she's aiming to improve the way children eat in popular family attractions, hotels, pubs and restaurants and her menus can be found in all the major theme parks including Alton Towers, Thorpe Park, Legoland, Chessington World of Adventure, Warwick Castle and Sea Life as well the UK's largest Holiday Park group – Haven Holidays and Butlins.

Her popular website www.annabelkarmel.com has more than 80,000 members, and her online TV channel www.annabelkarmel.tv offers parents recipes and a step-by-step guide to cooking healthy meals for babies and children.

Annabel writes regularly for national newspapers and magazines and also appears frequently on radio and television as the expert on child nutritional issues, including *BBC Breakfast*, GMTV, Sky News and Radio 2, 4 and 5 amongst others. She was recently voted as one of the eight iconic chefs of her generation for ITV's *This Morning*.

Annabel was awarded an MBE in June 2006 in the Queen's Birthday Honours List for her outstanding work in the field of child nutrition.

annabel karmel

www.annabelkarmel.com

acknowledgements

A big thank you to all our beautiful Princesses: Annabel Bennett our cover girl, Frankie Rushton Smith, Alba Hidalgo, Biba To, Betty To and Aemilia Cumberland.

I want to thank my wonderful team for all their hard work. Caroline Stearns for helping me develop the recipes, Dave King for his amazing photography, Smith & Gilmour for design, Seiko Hatfield my food stylist, Jo Harris for the fabulous props and styling, and Liz Thomas for make-up.

I also want to thank everyone at Ebury: Fiona Macintyre, Carey Smith, Sarah Lavelle, Sarah Bennie and Vicky Orchard.

A special thank you to Adrienne D'Souza, owner of 'A Party Palace' in 487–493 Upper Richmond Road West, East Sheen, London sw14 for lending us the stunning party props.

USEFUL WEBSITES
www.annabelkarmel.com

Kitchenware
www.lakeland.co.uk
www.wilton.com
www.cottagecooks.co.uk
www.kidscookshop.co.uk
www.thecookskitchen.com

Cake-making and decorating
www.squires-shop.com
www.cakecraftshop.co.uk
www.sugarshack.co.uk
www.cakescookiesandcraftsshop.co.uk

Specialist foods and sweets
www.cybercandy.co.uk

Accessories, decorations, partyware and tableware
www.mypartyparcel.co.uk
www.greatlittleparties.co.uk
www.partydelights.co.uk

Annabel Karmel's Complete Family Meal Planner
150 delicious recipes for children and adults alike
The essential follow-on to *New Complete Baby and Toddler Meal Planner*

Annabel Karmel Top 100 Finger Foods
100 quick and easy meals for a healthy, happy child
From the bestselling author of *Annabel Karmel's New Complete Baby and Toddler Meal Planner*

annabel karmel's after-school meal planner
'[Every] mother should have at least one of her books in the kitchen' *The Sunday Times*

annabel karmel the fussy eaters' recipe book

Healthy recipes specially developed for children from Annabel Karmel ...

I think it is very important to introduce children to a wide variety of tastes and flavours early on. I have created a range of delicious chilled meals based on favourite recipes from the world, including **Mild Chicken Tikka Masala and Rice** and **Chicken and Vegetable Noodles,** available from supermarkets. Tried and tested, and loved by children, they taste so delicious you'll want to eat them yourself!

Children love to cook too ...

And cooking is one of the most important life skills that a child can learn. Encourage your child to cook with one of my kids' baking sets – this exciting 12-piece Princess Baking Set will make a perfect gift. Getting children to cook is a great way to motivate fussy eaters. As well as learning basic cooking skills such as kneading, grating and separating eggs, through cooking children learn many other skills, such as maths, reading and writing and science, all without noticing. Inside each set, there are five recipes and all the utensils you'll need! *Available from all good retailers.*

Make delicious meals with my tasty cooking sauces and Dinosaur Pasta Shapes

Choose from **Tomato and Basil Sauce**, **Cherry Tomato and Mascarpone Cheese Sauce**, **Tomato and Sweet Potato in Moroccan Style Sauce** and a **Mild Fruit Curry Sauce**. Contribute to your child's five a day; simply mix with Annabel Karmel Dinosaur Pasta, cooked meat, chicken, fish, veg or rice. Alternatively, use a recipe in this book. *Available from supermarkets.*

Visit my website www.annabelkarmel.com **for more recipes, and** www.annabelkarmel.tv **for cooking videos**